Praise

'*Leader Awakened* sets out the ... achievement and the humar ... its endeavour. A very easy b——— to read, though paradoxically challenging as you find your mind wandering into self-reflection.'

> — **Sean Hastings, Chief Executive Officer of B2C Distribution**

'Samreen shows why taking the time to build on your strengths (underpinned by life's adversities) unlocks unhealthy patterns. This book has given me a deep and practical psychological vantage point and the inspiration to consider and reflect on how I work and live my life.'

> — **Morten Nilsson, Chief Executive Officer of BTPSM**

'Samreen demonstrates how leadership is not an approach that is architected; it stems from the intrinsic, grounded and core aspects of who I am and why, who I want to be and what this means for how I choose to lead others both professionally and in life.'

> — **Cilesta Van Doorn, Chief Marketing Officer of Global**

'As a second-generation British-Asian woman, I specifically related to Samreen's explanation of her childhood experiences and the impact this has had on her sense of identity. It has provoked me to question how my own identity impacts me at work more generally and as a leader.'

> — **Naureen Hussain, Director Data Estate of Virgin Media 02**

'Both humbling and thought provoking, *Leader Awakened* enabled me to relate my own personal journey to that of my professional behaviours. Putting theory into practice with Samreen is leading to significantly higher collaboration, trust and understanding in my team.'

— **Mike Hallam, Managing Director of Service Express UK and Europe**

'Samreen highlights the perils of an increasingly demanding backdrop fuelling stress amongst other consequences for leaders, bringing into clear focus the overlooked connection between body and mind. I am struck by her concept of "refracting" – a discipline – to slow down, to see, feel, think and then actually do something different when navigating these realities.'

— **Jagdip Panesar, Global Head of Learning and Leadership Development of Clifford Chance**

'A wonderful, thought-provoking resource for anyone looking to lead, form or reshape a senior team. This book brought to life how to put my purpose into perspective, understand the agendas of others, and develop a culture based on trust and positive relationships.'

— **Abby Thomas, Chief Executive Officer of Financial Ombudsman**

'A courageous approach that uses a powerful, raw and personal narrative alongside client stories to open up a dialogue.'

— **Wyn Francis, Chief Investment Officer of BTPSM**

'At the heart of this book is the deeply personal story of Samreen and her family. A story that will take you down to the depths, and then lift you up with relief. It's the personal that sets this work apart.'
— **Glenda Marchant, Executive Coach (former Publishing Director of *Stylist* magazine)**

'This book makes an important contribution to the literature on coaching and organisational development. At a time when leaders can be tempted with transactional strategies and illusory quick fixes, this book reminds us of the fundamental humanity at the heart of organisations.'
— **Simon Cavicchia, author of *The Theory and Practice of Relational Coaching – Complexity, Paradox and Integration***

'Like a good TED Talk, Samreen's book blends together personal story, practical examples and theoretical observations into a rich and compelling whole: a holistic exploration into the troubling complexities of contemporary leadership; a series of discrete investigations into various components of organisational experience; and an invitation into deep self-reflection about who you were, who you are, and who you want to become.'
— **Dr Richard Claydon, Chief Cognitive Officer of EQ Lab**

'I read *Leader Awakened* in three 90-minute sittings – the perfect length of book during busy times. It's helped me understand how all the facets of my life are intertwined to make "me" who I am.'
— **Carole Gilkes, Customer Director of Service Express UK and Europe**

'Samreen challenges us to accept that we all share a common truth – we all experience adversity or trauma to a greater or lesser extent. Short and elegant, hooked to the end, I expect to read this book two to three more times, and see it activate further changes for me each time.'

— **Ulrik Langermann, Leadership and Organisation Senior Advisor of Valesco**

'Samreen draws on the personal, the professional, the seen and unseen, the physical, emotional, psychological, physiological and social. There are different doors to go through, places to pause and reflect, and vantage points from which to look back from and then forward in one's own life as it has been and may possibly become.'

— **Anthony Kasozi, author of** *The Leadership Shadow: How to recognise and avoid derailment, hubris and overdrive*

'This is a masterclass in how to wear your heart on your sleeve well, how to look into the hardest times and keep going.'

— **John Higgins, author and researcher into speaking truth to power**

'If you can't have Samreen as your executive coach, this book is the next best thing, holding you to account for the changes you need to make.'

— **Megan Reitz, Professor of Leadership and Dialogue at Hult International Business School, author of** *Speak Up, Mind Time* **and** *Dialogue in Organisations*

LEADER AWAKENED

Why accepting adversity drives power and freedom

SAMREEN MCGREGOR

Find your inner compass!

Rethink

First published in Great Britain in 2022
by Rethink Press (www.rethinkpress.com)

Visuals by Candy Perry

Cover image © by Liuzishan

To Anees

You inspire me to be, and relish being, my whole self.

*May you awaken this in many more
people just by being you.*

Contents

Foreword

I used to think that hitting rock bottom was the worst thing that could happen to a person. And I can confirm that it is not fun. I lost part of my leg in a boating accident when I was 15, along with my dream of being an international rugby superstar. But I also discovered that there is a freedom that comes from having nothing left to lose. It can make you powerful and strong and dangerous, or it can destroy you. It is up to us to choose.

We will all experience trauma in our lifetime, and we all experience it differently. It is how we process our trauma that determines if we come back with new depth and wisdom, or if we lose a part of ourselves because we have to hide away what we're not yet ready, able to or willing to face.

I'll never forget speaking at a charity event in London when I was approached by a couple who were concerned for their 12-year-old daughter. Their concern was that her life was too safe: they had lots of money, they lived in a beautiful home and she went to a very expensive school. It's the life we all think we want, except this couple recognised that it is challenge and stretch that make us great and money cannot buy that.

The good news is we don't need to go out looking for challenge - it will always find us! The other good news is that we can choose how we respond to challenge, and this matters because it is a reflection of who we are and what we believe. Who we are and what we believe is important because it spills over into everything that we do. There is no such thing as a personal and professional divide.

I've been a professional athlete for 18 years, competing in four Paralympic Games. I've been the world champion and the world record holder. I've also experienced injury and defeat, and through it all I learned that who I am away from the athletics track impacts who I am on the track. When the pressure is on, our real selves come out.

As an executive coach working with leaders today, I experienced the same to be true in the world of business leadership. In Samreen's words, 'We cannot separate who we are from how we lead.' This is why it is so important to do the work of knowing who you are, being clear about your values, working through any unresolved adversities, and making more conscious choices. This book provides a great starting point.

Stef Reid, MBE
Paralympian, broadcaster, speaker and executive coach

Introduction

I'm a hopeless overachiever – similar to suffering from an addiction, admitting the condition is the first step to recovery (or at least living with it well). Ambition and a desire to do well, to be exceptional, are no bad thing – they are the wellspring from which so much good happens in the world. But ambition can, and does, come at a cost – especially when what lies behind that overachievement remains hidden.

Like any overplayed strength, ambition also has its shadow – and in many workplaces it is a habit that can be ruthlessly encouraged and exploited. That insatiable desire to push harder, do better and outperform the world can crowd out the space for internal reflection and prevent us from listening to the inconvenient voices inside that ask questions like: 'Is this worth it?' 'Why am I doing this?' 'What's happening in the rest of my life that doesn't fit with the language of achievement?'

I have worked for many years as an executive coach to leaders in all walks of life, helping them to navigate what feels like an increasingly impossible agenda filled with technical competence, exceptional performance, responsiveness to the unexpected and humble human connection. And I have been navigating my own life, which was complicated enough to start with as a Venezuelan/Indian/American/Pakistani/British 'citizen of everywhere', before then having to deal with my young son's life-threatening and gruelling illness.

I have written this book for anyone who is in or aspires to be in a leadership role. It explores what it takes to integrate the personal and professional, the manageable and the unmanageable – and the healthy and unhealthy demands we make of ourselves or others make of us. I have woven my own story, as well as those of others, into the book – because one of the things I know more than anything is that we cannot separate who we are from how we lead. This book expresses and shares the lenses I use after twenty-five years' experience in my profession, including the theory (psychological, neuroscientific, management science, naturopathic and body work) that supports and validates my interventions with clients. You will read stories from the coaching quarters that bring to life the adversities my clients have dared to face and chosen to transcend. You will discover what it takes to see the barriers that impede us from being who we are and realising our potential. You will see how the intrinsic and extrinsic environments we navigate play a role, and that it is possible to influence the journey and the outcomes.

I hope you gain insights from the resources and stories I share throughout the book, and these inspire you to take the space and prompts I offer at the end of the chapters to begin to adopt a new leadership development practice I call 'refracting'.

I contrast this to the act of 'reflecting', a concept which metaphorically relates a physics principle – which is what happens to light when it strikes a surface - to the process we use when we pause, notice ourselves, our thoughts, actions, and behaviours. In reflection, a ray of light simply *bounces back from a smooth surface*. In refraction, light enters different media (such as air, water or glass) causing a *distinct change in speed and direction*. The opportunity this presents enables you to understand yourself more deeply, scout out new angles, and to take actions to change the course of undesired behavioural and relationship patterns impacting you and others.

This book is a personal inquiry into my own development journey as a leader, professional and human being. It gives you the benefit of the ideas, theories, frames and lenses that have helped me to develop and apply resources for myself and my clients. The stories from the coaching room convey transformative shifts in the mindsets of my clients, how they view and work within their organisational systems and their behaviours. It is also intended to inspire you to see yourself as an instrument, to know yourself deeper, to wake up to the bigger picture and the behaviours and mindsets you can adapt to navigate your context even better as a leader and human being.

A contract with you, the reader

Throughout this book, I offer candid refractions I have made on significant experiences in my own life. All of these are real and personal. I expose critical moments that have presented opportunities for me to learn to traverse adversities. Many involve matters that are uncomfortable and some content may trigger distress. I believe I do not exist outside of the environment and dynamics described throughout this book. The work is deep and relational.

I also share reflections from coaching that provide tangible examples of others' experiences and circumstances, and how they faced them. The stories relating to clients are anonymised and I have sought permission for their inclusion in the book.

I have learned to navigate life and work-related situations, and I have the privilege of helping my clients do the same. Throughout this book, I attempt to catalyse a similar process for a wider audience, but to be successful this requires a similar investment and willingness for authenticity, honesty and brave reflection from the reader.

My outside-in perspective

Since I was a little girl, attending an American school and living in Caracas, Venezuela, I experienced life from the sidelines. I always felt like I was on the outside looking in. I was, and still am, a cultural exception. This has been difficult, but it has also given me a gift – the ability to observe with a sense of detachment.

Outside looking in

When I was invited for a sleepover at a friend's house, my parents would disapprove and say, 'You are not American, Samreen. Our rules are different, so you can't stay in the home of a family we don't know.' While I later realised this reflected their values around safety and control, at the time situations like this confused me and deepened my sense of being different from my friends. Despite Spanish being my mother tongue, my father encouraged me to speak only English. Research convinced him it wasn't good to raise a child learning more than one language because it delayed their development – a theory later disproved by evidence showing that learning several languages simultaneously leads to improved learning.

I interpreted this strict language rule as a signal that I wasn't Venezuelan. Although we travelled extensively to India and Pakistan to visit my father's side of our family, I didn't learn to speak Urdu or Hindi, so it seemed to me I wasn't Indian or Pakistani, either. I often asked my dad, 'If I'm not American or Venezuelan or Indian, then what am I?' He would reply, 'You are a global citizen, Samreen.'

I realise now that my father's global citizen classification was ahead of its time. In 2022, Guido Gianasso, PhD, Professor of Leadership at HEC Paris wrote a superb post about Emma Raducanu's astonishing grand slam win.[1] The post went viral and in just a few days attracted nine million views, thousands of likes and personal messages expressing the overwhelmingly familiar notion of being 'a citizen of everywhere' as reflected in Emma's diverse Canadian/Romanian/Chinese/British connections. There was an emotional outpouring from expats, internationals and transnationals, interracial couples and 'third-culture kids', all grateful for the acknowledgement of an overlooked world demographic.

I found comfort in hearing about others who go through life with similar questions about their identity, with a primal need to belong and who face the consequences of being different from a majority culture. The recent growth in awareness, engagement, curiosity and action towards embracing and inviting diversity, equity and inclusion is lighting up the stage for this much-needed dialogue.

As someone who has experienced a destabilising and complex journey, despite my gratitude for the growing support and curiosity towards generating better conditions for people to feel they belong I still find it challenging to open up about my lived experience. Writing this book marks a major milestone. When I reflect on the difficulties, I consider the stories I tell myself, am coloured by and project onto situations involving others, some of which we will explore together throughout this book.

Let's begin.

1
Accepting Adversity

Beaming a light to awaken you…

Acknowledging and understanding your relationship with trauma (and in all likelihood, you do have one) is necessary if you are to overcome its undesirable effects on you and those around you. Fusing personal, professional and academic insights to help initiate your liberation.

Abrupt awakening

'There is something very wrong, Samreen! Pack a bag. Go straight to Ward 7 at Stoke Mandeville – the paediatric ward. Take something for you and Darshan to sleep in. There is something *really* wrong. I don't know… See you there as soon as you can get there!'

exclaimed my husband, Fraser, on the phone. His voice shook, and I could feel the panic in his words.

'What did he say, Mummy, and why is he crying? I can hear him crying! Why is Daddy crying?' said my seven-year-old daughter Anees at 6:03pm on 4 April 2017, as I put the phone down.

I could feel her gaze penetrate mine while I tried to take a breath and snap out of my frozen state. I remember running around in a daze, packing random things in a bag and making Anees a chicken wrap that she didn't want to eat. Going into my son Darshan's room, I stared around aimlessly, not wanting to believe what was happening.

During the drive to the hospital, Anees fired a relentless stream of questions at me, and I desperately sought ways to relax us both. We comforted each other by squeezing each other's hands and taking long deep breaths together.

Within twenty-four hours, Fraser and I were taken into a room and told by a consultant that our nine-year-old son, Darshan, had a 'mass' in his brain, which was located mid-brain in the thalamus and was spilling into two ventricles. She said he was suffering from severe hydrocephalus, which she described as a build-up of fluid in the brain. They were going to blue light us to Oxford Radcliffe Children's Hospital in the next few minutes where our son would be seen urgently by the neurosurgical team.

As I write this chapter, the panic, terror, inability to think straight, and the relentless sensation of wanting to come up with answers and wake up from the nightmare flood back into my body. The mere thought of that day makes me feel cold and the unsettling sensations overwhelm me as I relive the traumatic experience in my mind.

I will never forget walking into the ward's teenage room and finding my tearful Anees with four identically photocopied images of Minions she had coloured in all on her own while Fraser and I were scrambling to support Darshan and guide our parents to the ward.

I will never forget the scream when the nurse inserted the first cannula into Darshan's small, pale hand.

I will never forget the neurosurgeon saying, 'Mr and Mrs McGregor, this is very concerning news. I must tell you that your son has a brain tumour – it's in the middle of his brain. We must operate immediately to take a sample and find out which of the one hundred and fifty-six tumours it is, to establish if it's treatable, and we need to carry out a procedure to release the fluid in his brain. There are considerable risks involved. We cannot operate until the full team we need is available, so we will have to wait two days.'

I will never forget looking into Darshan's eyes and realising that there was nothing I could do to influence his safety or survival even though I was his mother.

Trauma and post-traumatic stress disorder (PTSD) – a concerning trend

The American Psychological Association defines trauma as:

> 'an emotional response to a terrible event
> like an accident, rape, or natural disaster.
> Immediately after the event, it is typical to be
> in shock and denial. Longer-term reactions
> include unpredictable emotions, such as
> flashbacks, strained relationships and even
> physical symptoms like headaches or nausea.
> While these feelings are normal, some people
> have difficulty moving on with their lives.'[2]

Gabor Maté, the author of *When The Body Says No*, provided a different perspective when he examined the embodied effects of trauma:

> 'If trauma is defined as horrible things having
> happened to you in childhood… then it's true,
> not everyone is traumatised. But if you look
> at the origin of the word 'trauma', it's simply
> the Greek word for wounding. Trauma is a
> wound.'[3]

In 2017, the World Health Organization (WHO) carried out a world mental health survey to understand better the correlation between trauma and PTSD.[4] Of the respondents, 70.4% said they experienced lifetime traumas, and a clear correlation was found with people who suffered PTSD. The traumas with the highest proportions of PTSD were rape, other sexual assaults, and the unexpected death of a loved one. The study found that those with a history of trauma predicted both future risks of trauma and PTSD. In the UK, PTSD is not yet recognised as a disability, although it is in the US.

Our first encounters with safety and threat

Childhood is naturally the period during which we develop our sense of security and stability. Children whose families and homes lack these conditions must find their own ways of surviving and coping. These children tend to adopt learned behaviours such as being more mindful of others and masking their own needs and emotions. These tendencies, although helpful coping strategies at the time, can form barriers to building connections and trusting others, and can even impact people's ability to seek help and resources to fulfil their needs.

It is during childhood that we learn to regulate our emotions and interact with the world around us. Emotional regulation is an awareness and understanding of one's emotions and their impact on behaviour and the ability to manage those emotions.[5]

In the cognitive frame of how we view the world, social psychologist Ronnie Janoff-Bulman found that we form three generic assumptions in life, which are then reinforced during our lifetime: the world is benevolent, the world is meaningful, and I am worthy.[6] She believes that these underpin our wellbeing and equip us with the mindset to get through life's opportunities and adversities.

Our early relationships form the basis of our relationships throughout life. Attachment theory enlightened us to the importance of the people we attach to as children. Debates about its validity also help us to consider other formative relationships, for instance, infants develop these with their parents while adolescents tend to form them with their peers.

Stable and safe attachments are necessary conditions for us humans to develop our sense of self-worth and the belief that the world is a good place where positive things happen. The relationships we form and foster with our family, our friends, work colleagues and even acquaintances or strangers stem from these early bonds.

Studies have shown that adults whose childhoods involved relational trauma (severe breakdowns in their relationships) at home are more likely to suffer unhealthy relationships and more stress and anxiety.[7] Relational trauma is believed to manifest in later behaviour and adversely impact the ability to make and nurture healthy relationships.

We are learning from studies in epigenetics that our bodies respond to and store the effects of both loving and stressful interactions we have. This applies during childhood and over time. Traumatic memories have the potential to weave undesirable and damaging patterns into our psyche and body that can lead to recurring dysfunction in our relationships.

Our brain helps us to survive: learned behaviours of trauma

When we face a horrific situation and we are at a loss as to what to do, our response relies entirely on the most primitive part of the brain, the basal ganglia, which controls the innate and automatic self-preserving behaviours needed to survive. This part of the brain is also responsible for primitive activities such as feeding, escaping danger and reproducing.

The brain is a predictive organ and it learns from the consequences of what we do. It learns typical day-to-day behaviours from situations during our early developmental years. When we take a potentially unsafe action such as touching an electrical socket or crossing the road when a car is approaching and a guardian intercepts, informs us of the risk and offers an alternative action, the brain will learn and apply this categorically across a diverse set of situations involving danger and safety.

The brain gathers the data and understands that certain actions have certain consequences – this stems from our evolutionary survival needs. When our brain perceives danger, a threat or simply bad news, we tend to be guided by a negativity bias.[8] We register negativity far more easily but also tend to dwell on these circumstances far longer. Our memories of traumatic experiences stick with us far more than positive ones; we remember bad feedback more easily than good and we respond to and feel affected by adverse situations more strongly than desirable ones.

If your boss forcefully demands permission each time you want to try something new and responds negatively when you take the initiative without their blessing, a repetitive pattern of you acting in line with their expectations can be established. If you feel the need to know you are doing what is expected, your brain will ensure you follow this precedent in future situations (involving this boss as well as others).

In a professional context, these learned behaviours impact how we react to performance reviews, stakeholder interactions and interpersonal exchanges with team members or peers. The things that may once have kept us safe and helped us to survive can become the reasons for patterns in our relationships (more on this in Chapter 4).

The brain learns to expect a reality that isn't necessary or a reflection of what is happening in the moment and, as a result, it prepares for an emergency relating to a danger that may no longer be real.

Responding to imagined threat

Reacting to a danger that isn't there can have a detrimental impact on your work relationships. Your peers may perceive your behaviour as strange or irrational. You may be taking action to avoid a threat you can't quite articulate. The undesirable reality is that you are then seen as a difficult or awkward team member. An example I often see is unverbalised resistance from an individual out of a fear of rejection or the anticipation of negative consequences affecting them or their team members.

Snap judgments are common in the workplace when we don't have the space, awareness or time to understand what drives someone's lack of co-operation. This negatively impacts the quality of relationships and begins a repetitive pattern of interaction. It may lead to feelings of shame and individuals questioning their capabilities and contributions. The absence of dialogue reinforces these implicit and unspoken judgments, which leads to unquestioned norms and undermined connection and trust.

Learned behaviours drive the following undesirable effects:

1. Feeling defensive

2. Feeling judged

3. Having disproportionate reactions

4. Attending to the wants of others at the expense of our own needs

5. Avoiding personal expression and interaction

These undesirable effects impede interpersonal connection and shared understanding, and distort the relationship between people's intentions and the impact of their behaviour.

Trauma-induced interpersonal patterns

These undesirable effects lead to repetitive patterns in several contexts and relationships. A further complication is that the perception of time is based on lived experience and this varies between people. Time can be felt as fast, slow, short and long depending on the emotions and perceived experience of the individual. The implication is that the brain does not always know when the threat is over and when the primal fear response is no longer necessary. A traumatised mind is hypervigilant and programmed to wait for the danger to recur and then respond in the automated manner it has learned.

We need to find new strategies that help people feel safe and grounded at a deeper level – at the level of their nervous system – to stop the derailing of relationships they develop and grow in life. Paradoxically, it is through relationships that people can find strength, comfort and support to heal the wounds brought about by trauma. Without explicitly interrupting these invisible patterns, this opportunity remains latent.

REWRITING A NARRATIVE OF SELF-BELIEF

Tina was put forward for executive coaching by her boss because she demonstrated noteworthy technical potential and they hoped she would become the director of a senior in-house team. Tina was reticent and avoided the opportunity. It became clear that it wasn't a lack of drive that held her back but a lack of self-belief and self-esteem. When we began our work, Tina expressed that she was keen to unravel what was undermining her confidence and ability to take on challenges.

The early stages of our coaching work revealed dark and painful memories of her early school life when she was frequently bullied by a classmate. The bullying involved degrading situations, which included opening the bathroom stall while she was using the toilet and being laughed at and called a loser by the bully after Tina was selected to lead the debate team. Feeling threatened by the bully, she became fearful and pulled out of the debate team with trepidation that she would lose. Her continued academic excellence developed into a pattern of being on the receiving end of envy, and this affected her academic studies, work and social contexts.

Our work involved Tina facing the traumatic consequences of her history, accepting it as an unfortunate reality in her formative past, making space for her to process emotions such as anger at how she was treated and gradually rewriting the narrative in her current reality with validation from current examples of how her talents are valued.

In the coming chapters, we will explore how the unfolding reality faced by organisations presents unprecedented conditions for leaders and people today and generates a sense of getting or feeling stuck. We will consider how our ability to lead can be enriched by embracing and accepting (or being open to) associated emotional and physiological feelings relating to adversities and traumas we have faced during our lives. We will look at the importance of creating space to examine ourselves, our connections with others and the less obvious systemic and cultural dimensions that together comprise vital resources that maximise personal choice and agency.

Disrupting patterns by unleashing emotions

To enable people to transcend their traumas involves encouraging them to reflect on and assimilate the consequences of the specific adversities they have faced and to learn how to apply this enhanced consciousness. It also demands that people question their own reactions to the less comfortable emotions involved. This is easier said than done. There are environmental factors that make it difficult to create the time, especially in an organisational context (we will cover some of these contextual barriers in Chapter 5).

Also, the capabilities required are significant and specialised. Helping people to notice what underpins behavioural patterns informed by trauma requires skill, consideration and, in many cases, professional intuition. The expression of negative emotions that stem from trauma can at best get in the way of more functional and operational aspects of a work environment and at worst make people feel uncomfortable, judged and unable to cope. I do believe that it is important to address some of these requirements but they should not be reasons to avoid devising ways to surface and work with the effects of trauma.

Unlocking the need for control

Throughout his illness, Darshan struggled with the insertion of a cannula for blood tests and scans. He found the first few procedures severely traumatic and there was one occasion when the cannula was removed in a rushed manner and hurt him.

These experiences led to Darshan feeling the need to control his surrounding environment and conditions. In any procedure, he now insists on a countdown before a clinician is permitted to insert a cannula or begin a scan. This fear also crept into his need to try to control time: to be extremely early for school, swim practice, a race and even informal meet-ups with friends. By being early, he feels in control and able to positively influence the conditions surrounding his activities.

As parents, we encourage him to continue to use this approach as long as it feels helpful to him, but we also coach him to accept that there will be situations when he will not be able to influence conditions. It is important for him to experiment and gradually rely less on controlling the time and settings so he can embrace and normalise the uncertain and ambiguous conditions that he will inevitably face in life.

POSITIVITY IS NOT A LIGHT SWITCH

A Ukrainian client, Daryna, was facing considerable suffering as her family was affected by the events in her homeland. At a session that took place at the start of the Russia-Ukraine war, she described how many in her UK community, both at work and in social circles, expressed pity and encouraged her to 'look forward and remain positive'.

Employing a positive mindset when faced with painful adversity and focusing on hope can be remarkably powerful. This is backed scientifically by a growing neuroscientific understanding of how neurotransmitters like serotonin (which can be released through positive visualisation) can play an inhibitory role that helps to regulate emotions.[9] It isn't as simple, however, as turning a dial up or down and exerting control over how optimistic or pessimistic we feel in any given situation, especially when the limbic or mammalian layer of the brain responsible for emotions, learning and memory is activated by the reptilian layer on high alert to avoid danger. Ideally, the primate or human layer of the brain uses reason and logic to adopt the positive reframe, but a pre-requisite for this is that the reptilian brain is at peace and the mammalian brain is content. A more likely risk in this scenario is that heightened emotions are masked and therefore repressed. When I asked Daryna, 'How does looking forward and remaining positive feel for you right now?', she expressed despair, incompetence, frustration and helplessness.

Catharsis became the goal of our coaching session. I gently encouraged her to divulge the feelings, sensations and tensions she was holding in so tightly in an effort to spare others discomfort. The session involved long silences, tears and rage, and ended in elation. Her story triggered thoughts about my family in Venezuela who spent fifteen years living under an oppressive regime and suffered versions of what she described. I connected compassionately with her raw vulnerability as she released her pent-up remorse.

My intention was for her to use the space we shared to purge emotions. Soon after this catharsis, she could think more rationally about and articulate how to live with this reality that is outside of her control. She recontextualised the small and meaningful things she was able to do to offer realistic support to her family. We explored other things she could do to continue the process of purging emotion, like journaling, to lessen the effects. Weeks after the session, she was able to sleep better and felt less physically impaired by the intensity of the emotional burden she carried.

Our pain and anger are part of us too - make space for them

The detrimental impact of trauma on our bodies

My understanding of the body from my studies in bio-medicine so far leads me to believe that this phase in Daryna's life will contribute to what I would describe as a traumatic memory unit stored deep within her nervous system, organs, tissues and cells. As Gabor Maté expresses, 'Emotional competence is what we need to develop if we are to protect ourselves from the hidden stresses that create a risk to health, and it is what we need to regain if we are to heal.'[10]

What we have learned more recently is that when we frequently encounter stressful situations, our immune and stress response systems are compromised. This impacts the development of the immune system, manifesting as illness and diseases later in life. Even average degrees of anxiety and stress lead to autonomic responses, which trigger physiological responses like those we experience during a fight-freeze-flight response. You will read more about how these responses work in Chapter 8.

When a situation presents a threat, our pupils dilate to see more clearly and our senses are heightened to identify sources of danger. There is an increase in heart rate and blood pressure so that our muscles receive the oxygen and blood supply we need to move. The redirected blood flow leads to a cold sensation in the hands and feet, which stimulates a more rapid breathing pattern. As the sympathetic nervous system is triggered, we feel less pain. Stress hormones coursing through the body cause shaking and trembling, which is something my son still does years after his recovery in moments of distress.

Even in ordinary, everyday situations, our physiological response can be triggered disproportionately, depending on the degree of early or repressed trauma. Others may witness the response and interpret this as an overreaction or underreaction in the context. The correlation between trauma and physical pathologies and pain has been widely studied. Children with conditions such as chronic eczema have been found to have suffered traumatic conditions. In adults who suffer chronic pain or autoimmune illnesses, there may be a relationship between the pathologies and symptoms and an earlier trauma.

A study of over 17,000 participants, ranging in age from nineteen to ninety, looked at the transferral of trauma from childhood into adult life – labelled in 2000 as 'toxic stress'.[11] Researchers gathered medical histories of the participants' exposure to abuse, violence and impaired caregivers. Nearly 64% of participants experienced at least one exposure and, of those, 69% reported two or more incidents of childhood trauma. Results demonstrated a clear correlation between childhood trauma exposure, high-risk behaviours such as smoking and unprotected sex, and chronic illness such as heart disease and cancer, as well as early death.

The psychological effects of the COVID-19 pandemic

The Organisation for Economic Co-operation and Development's (OECD) Policy Responses to Coronavirus (COVID-19) compared results before and after 2020 and states:

> 'For decades, the prevalence of mental health conditions has been broadly unchanged; this trend changed in 2020 with the outbreak of the COVID-19 pandemic. From March 2020 onwards, the prevalence of anxiety and depression increased. This has sparked a trend in increased mental health risk factors involving financial security, unemployment, fear.'[12]

The following graph illustrates significant climbs in the prevalence of anxiety.

Trauma is proven to have long-term psychological and physiological effects, but the long-term impact of COVID at a mass level is still unknown. The pandemic has disrupted normal life, injecting all sorts of unsettling and unfamiliar circumstances. There have been ongoing waves of change and flux including where and how we work, whether children must attend school or be home-schooled and the planning of travel – adding all sorts of variable logistical tasks like testing, COVID passes and more. We lost our usual clarity of routine,

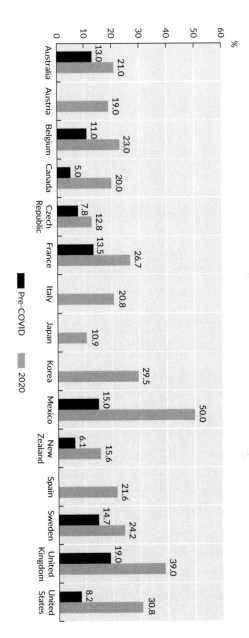

Significant rises in the prevalence of anxiety (OECD/2021)[13]

making people feel powerless. This led to a combination of physical and psychological adaptations to move through the unravelling pandemic landscape. We may talk about it more casually as we adjust to various 'new normals', but the mental and physical effects on adults and children are unpredictable. For some people, the pandemic has been a positive time with high levels of financial security, comfortable living conditions and more opportunities for rest, time with their family and replenishment. Many have expressed shame at this privilege, conscious that, for others, it has been a time of crisis, loss of loved ones or great danger leading to increased rates of domestic violence.

Talking to Healthline, psychiatrist Dr Julian Lagoy said:

'Generally, PTSD trauma is defined as being exposed to a traumatic event, such as a sexual assault, war, a car accident, or child abuse. However, the current COVID-19 pandemic has qualities that qualify as a traumatic experience as it takes a physical and emotional toll on many people.'[14]

Recent research indicates that healthcare workers, in particular, are experiencing unprecedented levels of trauma resulting from the pandemic and, while we don't yet have data about the trauma people experience outside healthcare settings, anecdotal reports suggest children and adults are experiencing mass trauma.

Bedding down

I am passionate about awakening others to see how we underestimate the effects of trauma. Trauma, as a concept, has its roots in the context of violence, uncontrollable disaster and death. Bessel van der Kolk, who wrote *The Body Keeps the Score*, expresses that 'the interesting thing about trauma is that people who suffer from it, want to forget about it because it [feels] too much [to handle].'[15] The adversities brought on by trauma are not a palatable subject. Van der Kolk has talked a lot about how unwilling many, if not most, people are to face and engage with the notion of trauma. Embracing trauma requires humans to accept that society and humans are profoundly irrational. Consider your own response to the title of this chapter before diving in: what preconceptions did you have?

Coming back to the deepest traumas I have experienced in my life, Darshan's cancer diagnosis, treatment and recovery top my list. For some, this example may feel a world away and difficult to imagine. For others, it may resonate more. In either scenario, there may be discomfort and a lack of willingness to even acknowledge its existence.

My learning has been that trauma is trauma – and every experience counts. Through my work coaching clients and teams, I have seen a rich tapestry of the threads of traumatic incidence sewn into each of my client's fabrics (and, in many cases, these are not recognised). Although there are relative differences and variations in the characteristics and perceived severity, each story I encounter has its roots in and associated human responses during and after events and traumatic memories.

I am on a journey to develop and crystalise how best to help a growing number of people embrace the work needed to hamper the undesirable effects this has on relationships, whether family, friendship or professional. I want to help people do the work to maximise their short- and long-term health prospects by understanding the physiological cost of avoidance and repression.

During the past four years, I have worked hard (with support) to not only permit myself to do the following, but also to make the time and create the space to:

1. Process what happened to me, my family and our life at my own pace – acknowledge and embrace the traumas, which often demands accepting less desirable situations and conflict.

2. Interrupt the automated cognitive responses my brain is so skilled at perpetuating, which have had a detrimental effect on my livelihood and relationships.

3. Stay with the pain (take some time to think about it and notice changes in my emotional state), accept the continued fear and discomfort that lessens very gradually but never quite goes away, realising that the shorter-term sensation of pain is not damaging.

4. Allow myself to be supported by practitioners who can help me determine ways of releasing the deep (and cumulative) effects of adversities and use processes to purge or extract them from my body, which gradually enables me to regulate myself, my emotions and somatic responses and my behaviour more effectively.

5. Seek naturopathic and integrative support to strengthen my health and wellbeing to help address the effects of trauma from a physiological angle (an arena I am only just starting to scratch the surface of in terms of my own learning and experience, which includes homeopathy and plant medicine).

6. Integrate the use of movement and exercise to support healing.

7. Continue learning, testing and finding ways to remain aware, mindful and holistic in how I navigate the road ahead.

In the intimacy of the coaching space, I notice that people often find it more comfortable to keep trauma out of everyday life. This is apparent in the organisations I work with and the judgments expressed by individuals in the professional as well as social and family contexts I roam. Studies on this topic by some of the greatest researchers and practitioners like van der Kolk validate this point. My work on myself and with clients has demonstrated that the most powerful route for people to transform what we learn from life's adversities is through acceptance, a willingness to face the trauma and be more conscious of its effects, and a curiosity about how to develop the capacity to work with it rather than put up with its hidden effects.

A SPACE FOR YOU TO REFRACT

1. What feelings does the word 'trauma' evoke in you?
2. Are there any events or circumstances that you might reclassify as traumas in your life having read this chapter?
3. How might their effects manifest in your family and social contexts?
4. How might these situations impact your behaviour in a professional setting?
5. How might they affect dynamics in a work context (for you and others)?
6. How do the effects of traumatic experiences show up in your or others' leadership?

2
Finding Flow

Beaming a light to awaken you...

Joy and fulfilment are rooted in moments when we willingly stretch ourselves beyond our perceived abilities, not when we stick to our comfort zone. Optimal experience is something that we make happen.

The concept of flow

Positive psychology is a modernist school of psychology whose starting point is human potential rather than mental disorder or deficiency (which was the focus of most twentieth-century psychological studies/theory). Positive psychology defines the concept of 'flow' as a mental and physical state during which a person experiences immersive joy, motivation and concentration. This leads to the individual being so absorbed that they lose a sense of themselves and their surrounding reality.

This concept has been researched extensively. Studies have validated the desirable aspects of individuals striving towards this state but also emphasise it as a means for organisations to maximise the opportunities for people to flourish and make meaningful contributions. Attaining flow is associated with having energy, gaining fulfilment and enhancing creativity and performance, or as Mihaly Csikszentmihalyi, a household name in positive psychology, said:

> 'When the self loses itself in a transcendent purpose – whether to write great poetry, craft beautiful furniture, understand the motions of the galaxies, or help children be happier – the self becomes largely invulnerable to the fears and setbacks of ordinary existence.'[16]

A necessary condition for flow, according to Csikszentmihalyi, who created the term, is that the level of challenge faced by an individual needs to be well-matched to the capabilities required to meet this challenge. To be in flow, we need to be challenged, yet also have the capacity and skills to address the challenge.[17]

Finding flow in my interactions with others

Drawing on the concept of flow, one life skill that I find tricky but hugely rewarding when I am successful is fostering connections with people. Working out how to be effective in my interactions has been central to my life at school, at work and with friends. I was made aware from a young age that mastering social exchanges is a necessary skill. It was an instrument to navigate diverse cultures given my international schooling, a necessary condition for me to traverse a big move from Venezuela to the UK at age fourteen and a pre-requisite to being an effective consultant and coach, but this aptitude did not come naturally to me. I consider today how hard I have had to work at it despite often being told it is an effortless strength of mine. I have memories backed up by diaries and journals of how anxiety-provoking and painful honing this skill has been for me.

Struggling to get into flow

Feeling stuck

I often hear from people that feeling stuck is a relatable sensation and that the contexts that present conditions for feeling stuck vary. Ironically, I too often feel stuck in my connections with other people. I feel a tug of war between two intense forces. On the one hand, I want to enhance my chances of being heard and, on the other, I want to protect myself from being hurt.

This tension has manifested itself in professional and personal situations in which I have been perceived to be less experienced or credible than those around me or where my culture and identity were considered different. The consequences have proven disabling for my self-esteem.

Psychological peril as a leader

A few years ago, I was appointed as the programme director of a leadership development programme for a family-owned food producer in the UK. The programme was designed to transition the business from a federalist leadership structure comprising individually run businesses with their own profit-and-loss statements to a more collaboratively led business, able to leverage its group structure. The executive boards of all the businesses participated. My aspirations for the programme were to design and bring to life an innovative and immersive experience that enabled its leaders to more skilfully navigate the shifting dynamics across their value chain and transform the business in line with customer demands and a changing marketplace.

I was given the role because of my expertise, experience and passion for developing leaders using creative learning approaches together with my humanist standpoint. Many would say I led the programme successfully, exceeding the expectations of the client organisation, but it was the least fulfilling experience I have had as a leader. What started as the opportunity of a lifetime ended in me relinquishing my ability to offer my full and true self.

I took on this leadership role when I returned from my second maternity leave. I lived by the narrative that I was not as capable or effective as others in the team. I felt I was too different. The impact was a loss of personal power and authority – to such an extent that one team member told the others I did not have the 'legitimate authority' to lead the programme. The vicious cycle that followed was one of me going through the motions. I maintained a professional veneer with the client and remained composed and collaborative with colleagues who were supportive, but I suffered severe anxiety and dreaded every session. At each team meeting, I felt a strong need to protect myself and control any behaviour that might expose anything those around me could judge unfavourably. My emotions were defensive, protective and, at times, shameful. I recoiled and retreated into myself. I didn't express what I saw, felt, thought or believed.

I suffered from a crippling dip in self-esteem and, in a professional context, as a leader or peer, this manifested in me avoiding verbal contributions, withdrawing and allowing this intense set of emotions and somatic sensations to grow internally. This stunted my energy and passion; I wasn't fully present and lost the opportunity to take part. I rejected the idea of bringing my whole self, which impeded the real gift of my contribution. The sad result was a sense of being excluded: that familiar, painful feeling that I differed from everyone around me, which left me in a hopeless, lonely and stuck place. Instead of claiming the space to express myself and influence the conditions, I counted down the time until we finished.

Reflecting back, I conclude that although I embraced the assignment believing I had the capability to lead the programme, the scale of the challenge I took on at that point in my life and profession outweighed my capability. Factors relating to the wider backdrop played a role too. As a result, I perpetuated my childhood narrative: 'I'm different; I don't belong; I'm not valued; my contribution is not worthy.'

Bedding down

As I have matured and become more skilled, I have gained the capacity to find, develop and use resources as a consultant, coach, parent and human being. I have reached out to people who have helped me surface the untested assumptions and a version of shame I have carried, by dissecting and nullifying its sources and adjusting my responses. The stories I share throughout this book shed light on these situations and how I have learned to reframe, adjust my sense of self and create conditions that engender flow in my interactions with people (both professionally and personally).

This might mean I am selective and discriminating about the conditions I will not accept and the choices this sometimes requires me to make. I have also seen, heard and shared intimate relational experiences of similar patterns I have witnessed when coaching clients on interpersonal (as well as other) challenges.

In the next chapter, we will explore why people get stuck in organisations and how to flourish rather than simply allowing conditions you might be unaware of to drain your power.

A SPACE FOR YOU TO REFRACT

1. What does flow feel like for you? Consider some examples.
2. Does the concept of 'feeling stuck' resonate with you? If so, in what contexts?
3. What can you learn from times you have experienced flow?

4. What are the implications of not finding flow in your life?

5. What are the consequences of this for you, for your wider context or for the organisation in which you work?

3
Stuck In Self-Sacrifice

Beaming a light to awaken you...

The seductive lure of corporate and societal quicksand can leave you 'stuck' in a harmful experience of apparently necessary self-sacrifice. Gaining sight and consciousness of this force will help you undermine its effects.

The backdrop

If you study a range of content related to leadership and strategy from the past fifteen years, you will see a developing narrative about the backdrop faced by organisations in the twenty-first century contrasted with the more predictable characteristics of the Industrial Revolution.

Industrial society has transitioned to an age of information, and knowledge workers and national economies are more intricately dependent on what happens economically on a global scale. There has been a move towards anticipating the future and needing to target longer-term goals, decentralisation and a transition from classic hierarchical power structures to more connected, fluid, knowledge-based, relational and organic networks.

I often hear C-suite executives use the term VUCA, which stands for a Volatile, Uncertain, Complex and Ambiguous world. This term was first used by the US Army War College in 1987 and published by Herbert Barber in 1991, developed from the work of economists Warren Bennis and Burt Nanus presented in their book, *Leaders: The Strategies for Taking Charge*.[18] It was later associated with the US response to the end of the Cold War and became a staple acronym in corporate dialogue and communication for how the world is different and what this means for leadership. CEOs, executive teams and organisations embrace the notion that in a VUCA world, agility is considered to be the critical mindset and capability for the fittest to survive.

The world is reeling from the pandemic, followed closely by complex economic dynamics such as fears of a recession similar to the 2008 market crash, a corresponding inflationary episode, the onset of the Russian-Ukrainian war, the fragmentation of economic and political unions as well as organisations making decisions and public statements relating to their allegiance and whether they choose to continue with or abort business ties given the political considerations. The conditions organisations face today are rapidly shifting and laced with fiscal, political, sociological, health and ecological consequences. Our humanistic experience of these macro-level dynamics is more immediate, raw and accelerated due to our access to information and the fake news offered by social media.

A world reinventing business models

Ploughing through complacent business models, assertive challenger organisations are breaking the mould in established industries. Some industries have operated in ways that no longer serve customers' evolving lifestyles, wants and needs. The required transformation involves breaking existing business models and incumbent product and service offerings that were the reason for profitable growth in a past era. Analogies like 'flying the plane while we build the engine' dominate the mindset and behaviours of Gen Y (Millennials) and Gen Z, whose purpose seems to be to break and reinvent industries.

With the onset of exponential access to data, analytics, artificial intelligence (AI) and robotics, the fierce race for organisations to reach their goals becomes their very reason for being, at a considerable cost to humanity. Besides the increasing demand to create a story around being purpose driven, which must be believable, it seems that traditional, hard-nosed ambition still drives market economies, shareholder expectations and the promise of financial gain. Equity stories that inflate the possibilities of growth and domination are frequently packaged as ethical, purposeful concepts. They are the link between the market-business-organisation dynamic and how it influences and feeds the ambitions of high-achieving people in corporate environments. This can lead to unfeasible achievement foci and fuel the underlying hubris and narcissism of some leaders.

A clash of needs

There is an inherent tension between the seductive reality of success and the primal need to protect financial stability and safety – to keep a roof over our heads and feed our families. Golden handcuffs (incentivised agreements that lock people in for specific periods) can hook and chain high achievers into committing to whatever it takes to perform and deliver, cultivating a sense of hopeless disempowerment and a need to put up with whatever is thrown at them while they wait it out.

We now face a mass of ambitious organisational paradigms demanding the fastest, best, biggest and most impressive, while driving individuals to perform even better. In the absence of true reflective thought and inquiry, those same individuals may become monsters in the machine and only later realise what has happened to them in their quest to satisfy their organisation and meet their personal goals. This realisation could lead to what we traditionally call a midlife crisis, but who knows what form it will take for future generations as the pace of development, expectations and possibilities continuously increases?

Monster in the mirror

This critical theme connects to the shadow side of leaders and teams, as well as to the consequences of the dynamics in the systemic view of organisations and their cultures. We shall explore this further in Chapters 6 and 7.

A life of paradox for leaders

The paradoxical nature of life as a leader demands a relentless work ethic but also an ability to maintain their wellbeing and quality of life. This presents as the drive to progress continuously yet the need to slow down, stop and learn from mistakes and failures. Mastery of their technical and functional expertise stems from a tenure of professional application and education but also a need to let go of what has become their comfort zone as they transition from doing to leading. There is an expectation to be ambitious and driven as an achiever yet have humility and compassion for the people around them. They are expected to have the courage to be accountable for tough calls and decisions and equally to embrace the vulnerabilities posed by the risks they take in the absence of certainty.

Leaders are required to behave in culturally acceptable ways, conforming to the norm, yet also to stand out from the crowd to gain recognition. There is an expectation to drive conditions that create harmony in their teams, yet also a responsibility to surface conflict and initiate the tough conversations that ruffle feathers. They need their team members to 'stay in their lanes' and perform their roles, yet also to collaborate and turn rivalry into having each other's backs.

Then there's the importance of creating space for diversity, nurturing differences with genuine curiosity, yet still asserting the need for performance and the delivery of desired results and challenging poor outcomes. If they are experienced and mature, leaders risk representing the legacy from the past rather than the freshness needed to reinvent now and in the future. The list of demands on leaders grows... and each demand contains a contradiction.

So how can a leader be their authentic self? It is a conundrum; it is confusing and draining to be pulled in opposing directions across multiple dimensions. It is also difficult to distinguish between what they need as a person, how that relates to their work, the contribution they make and how it fulfils their ambitions, values and desires.

BURNING THE JACKET

During a coaching chemistry session with a new client, Zara, who has spent her life working in academia, we explored her cynicism towards leadership development. Zara told me a story about the advice she was given during a course where she was encouraged to view her leadership as 'a jacket she can put on and take off' depending on the situation and people she leads. She expressed her discomfort with this analogy, stating that she dreaded being less herself and doing things that bore no resemblance to her true values.

She wanted coaching support to help take stock of the last couple of years during which she had navigated a tough organisational context and an adverse relationship with her line manager with whom she found it difficult to set and manage boundaries. This resulted in a period of burnout and a break from her work environment to recuperate. Despite this unmanageable phase, Zara secured a promotion and a significant elevation in her professional status and job title. Although motivated by exciting future-focused strategic deliverables, she was now constrained daily by limited resources. She was faced with constant compromises affecting project work and, in many instances, a cross-functional set-up demanded that she indirectly manage people (sometimes involving performance issues).

Fears of a return to unbearable levels of distress or further burnout made it important for her to find ways to navigate this context. She wanted space to 'burn the jacket' and work out who she really was so she could be herself more, skilfully and mindfully protect her own needs and continue to make the contributions she wanted to make without compromising her values.

Our time together was a space where she consciously examined the mechanics of choices she has made throughout her life. We also explored implicit, untested patterns that undermine her authority in a variety of tricky relationships she navigates as a leader and peer in her organisational context. Zara was also able to take a step back and look at the full scope of her management impact, allowing her to courageously challenge peers to step up and collaborate on shared goals and to stop overcompensating for their lack of participation.

Our work empowered her to make more deliberate choices and access a sense of personal agency and power she had not realised she possessed. It enabled her to reframe assumptions that held her back and hold colleagues to account when it came to collaboratively sharing the load. This has impacted her perceived influence, given her more freedom and is generating new possibilities for her. This did require Zara to take the jacket off and uncover more of herself.

The impact of a relentless pace: how leaders cope

The tendency is to do it all – to balance competing priorities and hedge your bets by keeping all bases covered. Leaders try to do it all without failing: maintain a resilient facade that is impenetrable to the inevitable blows that come with the need to deliver significant results, adapt to changing goalposts, make do with incomplete teams, capacity or capabilities and engage resistant shareholders.

Many organisations compromise quality in their quest to do too much. They fail to achieve results on costly initiatives, fall short of objectives and do not deliver the expected return on investment unless there is a clear focus. This is especially true given the finite time, resources and rapidly growing expectations of customers and consumers.

It is challenging to decipher what is important and urgent. In my experience, there is a demand for leaders to speed up and they expect their people to drive more outcomes and concentrate on their tasks. This creates a vicious circle, which requires people to do whatever it takes to deliver results in an unremitting dynamic that sweeps through the veins and arteries of our leaders, draining away their lifeblood.

This frantic pace generates a paradigm of constant action, which is detrimental to the quality of results and the health of the people at every level of the organisation. In 2019, the World Economic Forum reported some sobering statistics about the prevalence of anxiety globally.[19] According to the WEF's data, in 2019, an estimated 275 million people – about 4% of the world's population – suffered from an anxiety disorder. Anxiety disorders can present differently, but typical symptoms include:

1. Apprehension (eg feeling uneasy, worrying about the future, struggling to focus).

2. Motor tension (eg feeling restless, fidgety and physically tense, shaking).

3. Autonomic hyperactivity (eg feeling dizzy or faint, sweating, experiencing palpitations and rapid breathing, having abdominal pains).

Despite the continued encouragement from business schools, literature and discourse for leaders and managers to adopt espoused behaviours such as being purposeful, agile, humble and empathetic and model caring for their own and others' wellbeing, I continue to meet leaders who feel stuck. Whether they are caught in the relentless mechanics of the machine and lack the perspective to make changes or they are 'too busy' (which is paradoxically used as a valid reason not to slow down and question things that are no longer working) or they have burnt out, I witness too many leaders suffering versions of these undesirable effects. If our leaders get stuck in a cycle of trying to work out how to navigate the challenging context, racing between conflicting demands and maintaining a sense of self, what does this mean for wider organisational populations – our people?

Situationism (a term used by social psychologists) proposes that behaviour is an outcome of environmental factors that surround us, be it the culture of our organisations, the paradigm or collective mindset of our people or the opportunities and challenges faced by businesses. Is it a profitable business, feeding an ethos of abundance and possibility, or is it loss-making, fuelling a mentality of scarcity?

Dispositionism, which has its roots in Jungian psychology, suggests behaviours are a product of our innate attributes and personality preferences. Social psychology has evolved towards the notion that the environment and our personal traits are both valid segments of our behaviour. Early influences from my university studies in philosophy enlightened me to dialogues involving Socrates and his pupil Plato – whose frame was that the state controls the individual and the social context influences individuals' social responsibilities.

A neuroscientific lens on people's responses in this frenetic environment offers the view of the reptilian (most primitive) part of our brains – the part that, before we developed, was simply in place to keep us safe, as we explored in Chapter 1. The context faced by our leaders would suggest there is a predominant fight-or-flight need and response. A recent clarification of this theory is that there is a valid third response – a freeze stance, which suggests that people can experience a 'stuck' reality.

FEELING UNHEARD AND LOCKED IN

An executive team member of a multi-billion-pound international business going through a major transformation received a golden handcuff and, for monetary reasons, felt locked into the organisation and unable to leave.

She experienced a pattern of feeling unheard and pushed aside for valid strategic reasons but, rather than having open and honest conversations with her, her peers did things behind her back. She suffered ongoing pressure to deliver seemingly unachievable requirements despite being undermined and limited by decisions made by her peers that supported the strategic direction of the business but at a cost to the morale of the team.

While, on the surface, team members expressed positive intent at events at which they discussed their espoused values, in reality, implicitly dirty dynamics were rife within her peer group, making it a hostile work environment. This is an example of just how bad it can get when leaders feel stuck in an organisation.

Bedding down

The complex backdrop is evolving rapidly. Influences drive businesses to pursue big and arguably unviable ambitions, which stimulates individuals to seek satisfaction by subscribing to these dreams. The result is that countless leaders with whom I work are caught up in this dynamic with little or no ability to take a step back, notice what they feel, become aware of the impact on their health, reflect and question what needs to change. This provokes an image of a growing population of leaders and people who lack a sense of personal choice and agency and are sleepwalking into compromising situations. The long-term effects are damaging to the health and wellbeing of our people and organisations.

In the next chapter, we will explore how getting a holistic sense of our 'self' and integrating a deeper understanding is an important first step in orienting ourselves given this backdrop and resulting dynamics.

A SPACE FOR YOU TO REFRACT

1. Describe your energy as you read this chapter.
2. What tensions, forces and pulls did you relate to most as an employee, leader or professional?
3. Describe the pace and scale of ambition that your wider context brings you.
4. How often do you stop and question what underpins what you do (and choose to do) day-to-day, month-to-month, year-to-year and throughout your life journey?
5. On a scale of 1-10, how would you rate the state of your health?
6. On a scale of 1-10, how important is the state of your health to you?

7. What might enable you to understand or validate this rough assessment further?

8. What relationship is there between your work context and your health?

9. What insights have you gained?

4
Integrating The Whole

Beaming a light to awaken you…

Every individual is a beautifully complex being – physically, mentally and emotionally. Taking time and understanding how to embrace and unleash the entirety of our complex selves is as rewarding as it is challenging.

Roots of a self-reliant mindset

I have been driven and worked hard all my life. Looking back, I struggled to fulfil my and the perceived expectations of others. To be happy and fulfilled, I always aimed for notable achievements and to make a difference.

My parents are highly accomplished. My father left India when the rest of his family migrated to Pakistan following the Partition. He received a full scholarship from his engineering college for further studies in petroleum engineering at Stanford University in California. He travelled there by sea and completed his Master's in Science and gained a PhD in Petroleum Engineering. Within a year of his arrival, he met my mother, a Venezuelan, who also received a full scholarship to Stanford. She chose statistics because it was a new mathematical subject in desperate need of students. Capitalising on this gap, and as one of a handful of women students, she pushed her way through the channels to gain her qualifications and subsequently became a professor of statistics at Universidad Central de Venezuela. My mother faced tremendous adversity in her quest to improve her life – initially her father didn't support her choice to pursue an education and a profession, she didn't speak English when she received the scholarship to Stanford and she didn't have the funding to cover her travel and living costs.

Both my parents came from humble families with modest living standards. They are both from families with ten siblings and they shared a commitment to putting their younger family members through higher education and giving them the opportunity for a better life. They spent the 1960s to 1980s in Venezuela, working in the oil and gas industry during a period when the price of oil tripled. This, combined with their sheer determination and work ethic, enabled them to provide for their families.

Thanks to their hard work, my brother Shabbab and I grew up in comfortable conditions, empowered with choices and the freedom to pursue our ambitions. Venezuela is a country with blatant inequality and I appreciate my fortunate start. The view from the bedroom window of our apartment in Caracas was a beautiful mountain range covered in pastel-coloured shacks clustered in 'barrios' where the poor lived.

My need to push myself to achieve and secure financial stability is rooted deep within me. The drive to learn, develop and attain mastery – to excel in what I do – is what underpins my continuous reading, study, experimenting and practice. My father frequently coached me to understand and cherish the importance of these values. For years, this mindset has driven me to challenge myself at all costs, setting high targets and meeting or often exceeding them in my quest for fulfilment. This enabled me to push boundaries like winning the top dissertation award on my MSc, being the youngest to get promoted in my peer group, working full-time when my children were infants, excelling at my coaching work and commencing studies in naturopathic medicine in my late forties. This drive manifested itself in my desire to earn an abundant income to provide for my family or to support friends and other causes. To me, the ability to do this symbolises freedom and is my way of following my parents' example.

When I was fifteen, my mother advised me never to rely on a man and I took her advice until, in recent years, my son Darshan's significant health challenges and resulting treatment required me to focus on my family's wellbeing and stability from an emotional and spiritual, rather than financial, perspective. This deviation involved a learning curve that required me to let go of what I inherently believed defined my role and approach as a mother, wife and woman.

Two fundamental human needs

Something I learned from business philosopher Eliyahu Goldratt and my work with his daughter Efrat and others in the theory of constraints (TOC) community is that, at a basic level, humans crave happiness and fulfilment. We all share two foundational needs.

Know what you're choosing

The first is personal security and safety, which is covered by Maslow's hierarchy of needs.[20] The second equally vital need is satisfaction.

To play it safe, we stick to what is familiar, what we have grown comfortable with – the tried and tested approach to how we do things. We stick with the status quo, avoid change and try not to rock the boat.

To gain satisfaction, we are driven to explore unknown territory, pursue challenges, try something new – to disrupt, rock the boat and embrace change.

There is no apparent tension between the two needs until we consider the conflicting actions we take to fulfil them. To resourcefully address these conflicts and uncover ways to break through them, we need to explore what underpins our assumptions and values, and what drives the actions we take.

Self-awareness

Dr Tasha Eurich, the author of *Insight*, defines self-awareness as 'The ability to see ourselves clearly – to understand who we are, how others see us and how we fit into the world.'[21]

Building self-awareness is considered a core capability for people to be happy, fulfilled, have strong relationships and be authentic. My studies in organisational behaviour, neuroscience and management theory, combined with my experience in helping individuals understand themselves better, have shown me that the understanding of how to build self-awareness tends to be relatively shallow. There are enormous opportunities to go deeper.

Research over the past fifty years has addressed cognitive and emotional aspects. In the workplace, applied practice in generating self-awareness has focused on two core angles. The internal angle of self-awareness promotes the idea that we can all benefit from understanding our values, passions and aspirations, as well as our innate preferences and those that are environmentally influenced. Conversation-based exercises that encourage people to select and classify values they hold dear, and the expression of individual and group purpose statements, facilitate the exploration of these aspects in a work context. Psychometric instruments have been devised to give individuals insight into preferences and personality traits. This can provide data to consider how, through the lens of classifying traits, their experience and behaviour might compare with some generic categories. 'Extroversion and introversion' is a good example of the type of classification that helps individuals to notice more explicitly what energises them in interpersonal interactions and activities. This has provided a brilliant source of insight; a foundation to help people reflect on patterns in their behaviour and mindset and understand themselves better.

The external angle relates to how others perceive and experience people. Its value is in using insights from feedback to surface blind spots and find untapped potential. This feedback might be in the form of a quantitative 360 instrument or more qualitative inquiry-based approaches that encourage conversations or stories to bring the insights to life.

The added benefit of encouraging feedback practices is that they enable people in a work setting to see the world through the eyes of others. This requires that the process for and skill in delivering feedback are well designed and demonstrate integrity. I have seen situations where 360 feedback processes are used as a means to validate a subjective judgment made about performance.

Traversing the field of emotions

Deepening awareness also involves examining our emotions – what we feel and why. Data-driven insights and feedback from others provide a simplified sense of our strengths and the opportunities available to develop ourselves further. Being conscious of how the feedback makes us feel and our responses determines how we choose to use these insights – whether we decide to adopt a new mindset and try a different behaviour to reach our aspirations or enrich what we do.

But diving into the world of emotions requires an interest in and propensity for exploring undesirable sensations. Research professor Brené Brown has created a body of knowledge offering relatable stories about our need for and neglect of vulnerability and emotions. At the time of writing this book, a Google search of 'How many emotions are there?' gives a range of between four and 34,000 emotions, highlighting a significant variation in how emotions are defined. Brené's research involving 7,000 people over the age of five uncovers that the average number of emotions that people can classify is a mere three: sad, angry and happy.[22] Brené argues that being able to see and express emotions at a more granular level forms the basis of an important language that enables us to understand ourselves and each other through stories.

Having a language to help us explore this form of insight and data is hugely helpful. There is a growing need for the space to speak language and permission for individuals and groups in a society that struggles to embrace this conversation to process its consequences. We are at the early stages of this work.

TRANSCENDING LOSS

Trish is a female client who suffered severe trauma in her life when, after challenges conceiving, she gave birth to a stillborn baby. Subsequently, she was fortunate to have another child, but her husband suffered from depression for many years and they faced financial pressures. Trish returned to her job at a time when she needed to play a significant role in supporting the family financially.

Trish worked at an organisation that was going through a major merger followed by a demerger. Initially, our coaching was around her embracing that her 'assumptive world' was devastated by the trauma of giving birth to a stillborn baby, her husband's depression and feeling like she had to hold it all together. The need to perform and show up professionally was an expectation she grappled with, having deep and painful wounds, and the circumstances demanded growing levels of resilience. The organisational context brought about sharp changes to the nature of the role and function she had previously performed. This triggered personal insecurities about her capabilities.

Our work gave her the space to feel heard and helped her to stay with the emotional and physical pain rather than attempting to hide from it. We worked on gently reframing aspects that could help her heal in her own time and feel more in control. The coaching provided her with resources that she drew upon at her own pace to build her confidence while she continued to manage her challenging circumstances at work and home.

I witnessed a subtle and gradual release of the trauma, helped by Trish increasing her interactions with extended family and friends and embracing more support from others. Within a year, Trish was pregnant with her second child.

Adding layers to self-awareness

I have learned that although the established sources of self-awareness I have briefly outlined are good and necessary, they do not provide a holistic picture. Moving into some of the neuroscientific regions of our behavioural patterns has brought to the fore how critical it is to consider what drives our deeper needs for satisfaction and security when viewing some of the more surface traits and characteristics that form part of our personality, behaviour and perspective.

My studies in biomedicine, nutrition, mindfulness, somatics and embodiment continue to enlighten me to a world of study that has also progressed, but sadly in parallel to, rather than in connection with, our self-awareness at a more cognitive and emotive level.

Dualism – understanding the parts but missing the whole

'The part can never be well unless the whole is well.'[23] Plato's point supports my personal fascination with how the medical domain has evolved from the concept of dualism, which is underpinned by the belief that the mind and body are not connected. Infused with reductionist scientific theory, dualism is an approach that led the medical profession to study, examine and treat the mind and body separately, which served us well during the Industrial Revolution when more mechanistic approaches to learning prevailed. However, it ignores the impact our environment has on us.

Gabor Maté, in his book *When the Body Says No*, explains simply, 'Stress is a response to a perceived threat that affects every system in our body.'[24] Through a combination of my understanding of how our endocrine system works and my consultations with integrative medicine specialists when I experienced chronic pain symptoms, I learned powerful and counterintuitive insights about the relationship between stress and wellbeing. I became more holistically curious about aspects beyond my values, personality traits, drivers and emotions and how combining this with physiological factors can enable different possibilities for safeguarding health, preventing illness and addressing pathologies. I plan to rapidly extend my learning and practice to encompass this field over the coming years. I am already exploring ways to tackle the physiological manifestation of a pattern of chronic stress. I will touch more on this subject in later chapters.

A physiological perspective on repetitive stress responses

When we perceive a threat, our hypothalamus triggers an endocrine pathway as a regulative response. A hormone called corticotropin-releasing hormone (CRH) is released, stimulating the pituitary gland to release another hormone called adrenocorticotropin (ACTH) into our adrenal glands and the fatty tissue just above our kidneys. This triggers the production of cortisol, which floods the blood supply in our body with glucose that serves as an immediate energy source to mobilise our muscles, readying us to confront or run away from the threat.

In chronically stressed people like me, this pathway is triggered regularly, meaning that cortisol is produced more frequently than needed. Over time, cortisol destroys tissues, raises our blood pressure and can damage organs like our heart. Cortisol can also have a suppressant effect on our immune system. Growing research into the presence of cortisol shows it has a detrimental effect on our natural killer cells, such as T-cells, which have a remarkable ability to protect our bodies from foreign intruders like viruses and destroy or prevent the growth of malignant abnormal cells.

When a threat response is triggered in situations where this pathway is unnecessary or overstimulated, there are both short- and long-term damaging effects. These can lead to physiological conditions such as a suppressed immune system, organ damage, autoimmune diseases and even cancers.

Creating space to be mindful

Meditation, although practised for centuries in the Eastern world, has auspiciously grown in popularity in Western society and is proving a powerful instrument to nurture self-awareness. The practice is increasingly used to help adopt a healthier lifestyle, regulate emotions to counter stress and anxiety, enhance sleep and rest, and manage pain.[25] A rapidly growing repertoire of mindfulness practices can be used to support stress, anxiety and depression. Evidence of its impact on the central, peripheral and autonomic nervous systems is mounting.[26]

I encourage my clients to experiment with meditation and alternative practices, however, I see (myself and many) people caught up in a rhythm of life that follows a rapid drum beat powered by human-made expectations focused on producing outcomes. We live in a world that values what gets done and misses the richness and benefit of creating space to decompress, assimilate, clarify and question.

A simple way in which I encourage leaders to generate a more mindful space for themselves and with others is by taking small steps to integrate nature into their day-to-day lives. Taking breaks that combine fresh air and walking stimulates the body and brain in a different way – interrupting the intensity of operational activity and infusing the body with movement.

We will touch on the desirable impact of mindfulness for leaders and teams in Chapter 5.

FROM PARALYSIS TO PROMOTION

Francisco, a C-suite executive referred to me for coaching, presented with high levels of stress and a recent diagnosis of Bell's palsy, a temporary paralysis of the face. While doing a leadership development programme, it became clear that although he was a bright, accomplished and effective leader who was valued, he struggled with some difficult dynamics, which impacted his ability to maintain a healthy family life.

We journeyed through what he needed to see and do differently to address the cause of his symptoms and enjoy more harmonious family time without compromising his passion and commitment to his work.

A significant aspect of the work involved Francisco understanding the unspoken conflicts and power games he experienced with stakeholders. Through our coaching, he could reflect, articulate and share emotional surges and, within a mindful space, work out how to detach himself sufficiently to co-author better interactions and outcomes with tough stakeholders. This unburdened him of unhealthy attachments. We developed the skills he needed to manage boundaries and use compassion and logic to find avenues through which he and these stakeholders could approach things differently. His health dramatically improved, his sense of control grew, his wellbeing flourished and he was promoted to an even bigger role that aligned with these aspirations.

Bedding down

Coming back to my life story, I am thankful for my mother's encouragement to be self-reliant and independent, but I am also thoughtful about the impact this had on my relentless work ethic and blinkered determination. Many people who know me and my work have described me as successful and there are times when I am humbled and proud of the progress I have made in line with the evolving expression of my goals and ambitions. The impact on my health, however, is clear: I have traversed periods of depression when my achievements fell short of what I felt was my potential. I have suffered chronic neck pain that has worsened and I have managed a thyroid autoimmune illness through naturopathic means. More recently, I have learned that the excess (and unwanted) fat I carry around my waist may be influenced by the levels of cortisol I produce.

The invitation to you, the reader, is to be aware that there are numerous dimensions and facets to generating self-awareness and value in integrating these through conscious and embodied ways. I introduced the concept of 'refraction' at the start of this book to encourage you to seek a deeper understanding of yourself and provoke shifts in your thinking and behaviour. The list is not exhaustive but some aspects I have been meditating on more consciously to better understand my 'self' and expand this sense of self-awareness include:

1. What am I conscious about and what might I be less conscious of – and how can I find ways to access and reveal more of the unconscious?

2. What is reptilian and primitive and designed to keep me safe, what is mammalian, needing time and space to gain acceptance, and what has evolved for me as a primate to which I can apply reason and logic?

3. My mind, brain, cognition and more rational approaches are useful instruments, but when might they be best integrated with other modes?

4. My emotional, more felt aspects and manifestations (we will explore some of this in the next chapter) offer critical data and skills.

5. My body, biological aspects, physiological signs and perhaps less visible processes that remain unseen until something goes wrong.

6. My experience, memories and the stories my mind and body are able (and willing) to interpret, store and learn for re-use or questioning in the future.

In the next chapters, we will travel through stories and concepts that transition our awareness from the internal, intrinsic facets listed above towards a bigger picture connecting the self with others, the systems we inhabit and the cultures that are formed around and influence these connections and us as individuals.

A SPACE FOR YOU TO REFRACT

1. Reflect on pivotal moments in your life.
2. Who has influenced your life story? How?
3. What generates a sense of personal security for you? How important is this to you?

4. What drives you, feels fulfilling and generates a sense of satisfaction?

5. What compromises do you see yourself making in life?

6. On a scale of 1-10, how self-aware are you?

7. What new vantage points might you have after reading this chapter?

5
Cultivating Connection

Beaming a light to awaken you...

Families, educational institutions, social settings and places of work are all social constructs. Your experience of those environments will be determined by the quality of your connections and with whom you share them.

A dream team to captain

Four years after my son Darshan's cancer diagnosis, he was made captain of the swim team, which was awesome because one of the side effects of the experience was losing all of his social connections. Lots of wonderful friends supported him during the crisis, but no one would expect ten-year-old children to have the maturity to understand what he went through and how the experience fundamentally changed him.

A computer game called *Fortnite*, which involved killing, was incredibly popular at the time and Darshan's peers socialised through playing this game. Darshan wanted nothing to do with video games and *Fortnite* in particular. He just could not relate to it so he became isolated. This was the worst thing that could have happened during that difficult period when Darshan was trying to reintegrate into school life and shake off the trauma of what he had been through.

Before cancer, he was a keen swimmer so I suggested he take it up again. He resisted at first – he feared failure because he had missed a year and a half of practice. After some gentle coaxing, he agreed to give it a go with no expectations. Thankfully, he recalled that being in the water had relieved the pressure of his severe headaches before his treatment and the memory triggered a positive association.

He became a strong swimmer, but then we entered lockdown and the pools closed. He was lost and angry. I said that we could do some Zoom sessions with a personal trainer I know so that he would be fit when lockdown ended and he was free to get back in the pool. He loved those sessions so much that we do strength training together several times a week and his swimming has exponentially improved to the point that he has skipped two group levels.

One evening after swimming, he excitedly told me that the other pool had been over-chlorinated, so the entire club swam together in his level's pool.

Four of the higher-group swimmers told Darshan they thought he belonged in their group level. After all he had been through and having almost given up swimming, it was the most gratifying progress. The camaraderie among the swimmers, especially the older and the younger kids, is heart-warming. Darshan encourages those who lack confidence to go for one hundred butterfly strokes and they achieve it. He has learned this encouragement from his older role models.

One boy on the team asked Darshan why he did not swim with them for a year and a half. Although he rarely talks about his illness, he opened up and told the boy about it. Slowly others in the club grew to learn Darshan's story through a combination of him sharing and them asking him about his cancer. The conversations he has in between swims at practices, when they catch up about what is happening at their schools and in life, create a sense of trust, care and camaraderie. He feels his teammates look after him and he is a valued member of the club.

It is so comforting to see him blossom as a captain. He has been praised by the coach for impacting the team's collective accountability for winning and excelling but also for bringing a rare fragility that has deepened relationships and team culture. When asked to describe the team he captains, he said: 'We all talk to each other as if we are a family and feel connected. We shout the loudest out of all teams at galas! We all want each other to do well, and that is all that matters. It is a dream team for me to captain.'

Understanding human behaviour

A single explanation for the dynamics and intricacies of human behaviour does not exist. I have found that psychology has brought an academic basis to my experience of people's perceptions, personalities and behaviour. The British Psychological Society (BPS) defines psychology as 'the scientific study of the mind and how it dictates and influences our behaviour, from communication and memory to thought and emotion'.[27] Classically, I have seen it described as being concerned with individuals, but over the years this has extended to an organisational context.

Looking at humans through a psychological lens allows us to see and study emotional activity, what is conscious and unconscious, sensory experience, thinking processes, perception and memory, albeit with an inevitable level of subjectivity and assumption. When I reflect on my schooling and development in this field (which has been a combination of university studies, organisational behaviour-framed content learned in a professional context, psychotherapy and counselling) and wider, more systemic approaches or interfaces, I consider the application of this science in the world of work.

I encourage my clients to be curious about and aware of the various attempts to explain behaviour throughout the history of psychology. These range from more definitive approaches, like scientific methods involving biological and behavioural aspects, to imprecise elements involving less tangible studies and interpretation. In my work with clients, through conversations and exploration, these diverse attempts aimed at explaining behaviour offer a useful language, vantage point and opportunity to generate shared meaning.

A high-level chronology of psychological perspectives

Structuralism, a school of psychology introduced by Wilhelm Wundt and then further developed by Edward Titchener, is considered the school of psychology in which the concept of introspection was born. It focuses on the concept of conscious awareness – looking at and becoming conscious of our behaviours.

Functionalism stems from the organising principles of Darwinism and puts forward the idea that the mental and behavioural processes involved in natural selection and the evolution of humans enabled us to adapt and respond to the system within which we play a role.

Psychoanalysis is the school famously associated with Sigmund Freud. It views behaviour as the manifestation of 'repressed' and 'unconscious' rivalries and conflicts and aims to surface these unconscious factors with patients.

Psychodynamics is a descendent of psychoanalysis. It proposes the concept that early life experiences are the roots of our unconscious and have a significant influence on our perspective.

Behaviourism introduced the concept of seeing our behaviours as responses to environmental stimuli, a process called 'conditioning' famously evidenced by Pavlov's experiments showing how obedience could be developed through the provision of rewards to dogs.

Humanistic school looks at behaviour through the lenses of the person exhibiting the behaviour rather than the observer. It adopts the notion that not all behaviour is determined by people's environment and society and that people are in control of their lives and have 'free will'. Gestalt therapy, a therapeutic approach that focuses on being mindful and noticing the 'whole', broke away from its psychoanalytic roots and influenced more Humanistic philosophies which see the whole as being greater than the sum of its parts and steers us away from being reductionist in our perspective, as some of the more 'scientific' approaches encourage. This is an approach focused on the present rather than beginning with the past like the work of more analytical schools.

Cognitive school is the scientific study of the brain, likening it to an information processor, which has enabled an understanding of how we create, store and recall memories. This school has interfaced closely with neuroscience and, in more recent years, has examined the science of how humans think.

Social psychology studies the interpersonal behaviour of individuals in their social situations. It is founded on the idea that all behaviours occur in a social context. There is an important element of how people relate to one another, including in organisational life.

The existence of other people is a major influence on people's behaviours, thought processes and emotions, and how organisational culture forms and coalesces.

A sociological lens encourages us to understand individuals within their social context and how they co-exist. Ultimately, organisations are social contexts. Human interactions and interpersonal relationships in the social environment influence and are influenced by less visible dynamics between feelings, actions, decisions, emotions and even the flow of energy.

Taking a step back and considering perspectives within a given context has helped me to understand and support clients in acknowledging why people do things and what underpins or drives their mind-set and behaviours at a deeper level. When we make assumptions about and judge people's behaviours or actions without taking into account their context (some of which may be obscured), it is called 'fundamental attribution error'.

The consequence of this limitation is that, in the fast-paced world we inhabit, humans can lose sight of the bigger picture, be blinded by singular and individualistic frames and only see an incomplete picture of themselves and others. In my experience of working with people, this is a significant limiting factor in how we go about generating, managing and nurturing our relationships. An example might be an experienced professional who takes on a less senior role to accommodate competing needs stemming from family circumstances, such as a single mother who needs to work but also balance childcare. This professional might be treated as a novice or given less authority even though her capability is superior to what is expected of her and the resulting reward and recognition.

We are social animals

Aristotle said, 'Man is by nature a social animal; an individual who is unsocial naturally and not accidentally is either beneath our notice or more than human. Society is something that precedes the individual.'[28]

Offering a cognitive perspective in his book, *Social: Why our brains are wired to connect*, Matthew Lieberman explains how neuroscience surfaces our social reasoning, which is separate from the system we use for nonsocial thinking, and each of these works in isolation.[29] He describes our social system as doing three things: connecting us with others, determining whether we belong (are accepted or rejected) and whether we feel pleasure or pain. As we learn through our social interactions, there is a predictive element. Through our intuition, we determine what helps us to connect – to interact and achieve coherence, harmony and manage tensions in our relationships. As humans, we perceive an important evolution in the languages, cultures and tribes we have developed and grown. Connections we make as a result involve how we communicate, negotiate and collaborate.

Connections to the system we inhabit

How we function has evolved from our hunter-gatherer days when some humans hunted and others cultivated fruits or gathered plants, made clothing, produced the tools and nurtured the children. This division of labour has evolved given the more highly populated, complex and technologically enabled world we live in but still applies today. Shops, retailers and, increasingly, digital businesses drive change in consumer behaviour. For example, Just Eat, the food delivery service, fulfils the role of hunting and gathering in modern society, giving a convenience-based and scaled ability to satisfy basic human needs such as how we get our food.

I would argue this poses an equal if not greater need to be clear about what underpins and influences how we collaborate and connect, particularly in a world that is opening its eyes to decades, if not centuries, of negligence and environmental consequences.

Dynamics of bonds and connections

Strong emotional and physical bonds with caregivers during our formative years and, in particular, a primary caregiver, have been shown to influence relationships later in life. Some of these studies have shown that trust and mutual engagement are higher among people who have developed stronger attachments in formative years.

Bowlby proposed the attachment behavioural system where human infants have developed innate attachment behaviours to develop proximity and get support from attachment figures – those they depend on for protection from physical and psychological threats from the surrounding environment.[30] His studies involved observing infants separated from their mothers and a pattern of reactions involving crying, clinging or seeking to find them. Bowlby observed from his various studies that an attachment behaviour system affects the relationships, emotion regulation and personalities of people as they mature through life. In the 1980s, Hazen and Shaver progressed these studies by looking at how the nature of infant-caregiver relationships correlated directly with dynamics of safety and security in adult romantic relationships.[31]

Both biological and physical sciences have introduced ways for us to understand ourselves as part of the animal kingdom and as primates. Like all other primates, we are animals who lead long lives and cultivate long-term social bonds through affiliative means, such as using our hands and exchanging touch. As we have evolved, social touch has become the basis for the trust, dependence, protection and development needed for wellbeing and reproductive success.

When I relate the above ideas about our relational reality – how we connect and form bonds as children and then as adults in the context of an organisation, as well as in my work with teams – I reflect on the conditions, characteristics and processes that are needed to support people, leaders, groups and teams to develop trust and a shared sense of positive intent.

In a team context, I encourage people to use story-telling as a means to better understand each other's life influences, values, mindsets and behaviours. This requires me to use my psychotherapeutic training to apply careful and considered design principles to create psychological safety and facilitate nuanced human dynamics in an intimate and purposeful setting.

Defensive mechanisms

There are less conscious processes involving defence mechanisms that enable individuals to conceal ways they use to feel safe. Anna Freud defined these defence mechanisms as 'unconscious resources used by the ego' to decrease internal stress.[32]

Some examples include:

1. Denial: refusing to recognise an experience that feels too difficult to face, such as a spouse caught in a violent relationship refusing to accept that their partner is abusive.

2. Projection: a tendency to displace inner impulses or unwanted feelings and perceived inadequacies onto other people. Think of someone whom you dislike or hate. A projection would be holding the belief that they dislike or hate you.

3. Avoidance: dismissing thoughts or feelings, or not engaging with people, places or situations to circumvent discomfort. Failing to show up to a social event, for instance, or even minimising the use of eye contact and lowering your voice.

4. Identification: changing facets of behaviours to appear like another person without consciously realising. In a meeting where an individual adopts a similar body language to their boss.

5. Regression: reverting to a younger phase of development where less demanding behaviours offer protection from the current situation. A toddler, for instance, displays behaviours present at an earlier time such as sucking their thumb or soiling their underwear.

6. Sublimation: use of a productive outlet to attend to conflictive emotions or unmet needs. When you have an intense day at work and finish the day by exhausting yourself through high-intensity exercise.

7. Dissociation: disconnecting the mind from the body or environment to distance yourself from memories, emotions, thoughts, feelings and

even your own identity to avoid overwhelm or stress. This can be a powerful weapon used to escape the effects of trauma. Consider whether you have ever been reminded about an event or period in your life and realised you had forgotten it completely.

8. Reaction formation: replacing your initial impulse towards a situation or idea with the opposite impulse. In younger years, where a child (often associated with prepubescent boys) is attracted to someone but expresses hostility instead of appreciation to avoid confronting these romantic sensations.

9. Humour: numbing negative emotions associated with a situation by resorting to a joke or funny interpretation. This is one I see often in a corporate context where it feels easier to swerve a difficult emotion or topic by cracking a joke and diffusing the discomfort.

In a team context, these subtle and, in some cases, deeply entrenched mechanisms can interfere with and inhibit purposeful connection, particularly where people are unaware of these phenomena and their implications. Skilfully facilitated storytelling can generate a level of awareness of some of these mechanisms and patterns of psychological defence behaviours within the team in a safe and appreciative way and generate more conscious aptitudes about how to work with them.

STORIES TO CONNECT US AND OUR WORK

I triggered the transformation of a team I coached by simply asking them to share their life stories to enable their colleagues to understand who they are, connect on a personal level and build mutual empathy. I encouraged them to choose how much to share but to be honest and authentic about people who influenced them and inflexion points throughout their lives.

Everyone went through the exercise and the team's leader, Aera, shared an extraordinary story about her damaging gambling addiction for many years. This is a leader who revealed aspects about herself and her life she had not declared to many others. She shared how she remembered having a conversation with herself on a park bench and saying, 'You have got to sort this out. You've got a choice: are you going to sort it out or not?' She chose to sort it out and now she's a highly respected, senior director in a multibillion-pound business, leading a breakthrough transformation.

The impact of Aera baring what felt to me like a nude form of vulnerability was that the team gained common ground. All members felt able to explore their imperfections – leading to a striking sense of total equality. Although Aera told me later that the story wasn't a defining moment in her career, and she was getting on relatively well despite what was going on with her, what she realised as she told her story is that 'everyone is soldiering through their corporate lives carrying a lot of personal baggage, and the ability to reconcile and deal with these adversities is harder for some than for others. Being cognisant of this is so important as a leader.'

At the end of the two-day session, they all agreed on how they were going to truly seek to understand each other's needs and approaches in their day-to-day work context. They also wanted to challenge each other more, which meant leveraging the trust they generated in this rare space together. This would be possible if they could sustain a new shared assumptive base of positive intent and a deep appreciation and care for each other at a human level.

The functional aspect of this team requires them to operate in autonomous ways across a value chain, playing a critical role in serving stakeholders habituated to a traditionally siloed and hierarchical environment, and to transition the organisation to be seen and operate as a rapidly evolving flexible ecosystem. In supporting this complex context, the teams work across multiple projects simultaneously and often find themselves dragged into specific project areas, making it easy to lose sight of the bigger picture and the business's interdependencies.

Aera describes the outcome of our work as having enabled each of her team members to step back from the purely transactional relationships and use empathy as an instrument to combat the friction spawned by this complex and political environment. This subtle shift in their relationships as a team meant that they were able to avoid spending time speculating about or second-guessing each other's motivations or intentions and instead focus on getting work done collaboratively. They described the subsequent connections they strengthened over time as based on mutual care and trust.

For this work to be done effectively, a grasp of the handling of emotions is critical. My experience with many teams over the years evidences a powerful opportunity to enable individuals, in a supporting and challenging context, to work with and relinquish the (less conscious) defensive mechanisms that human beings develop to grapple with perceived threats outlined above.

We are schooled and measured individually

Before even getting into the organisational setting, one small but noteworthy observation about how individuals integrate into an organisational context is the transition from education to profession. Throughout our schooling, the education system wears a predominantly individual lens – there is a reductionist approach to teaching content and assessing capabilities. This is understandable as it would be difficult to enable us to individually learn given our differences in learning styles, preferences and rates of learning. My son is an avid mathematician who spends hours looking at, deciphering and practising algebraic equations at his highly academic British grammar school. My daughter struggles with maths and, although she works hard, she cannot match my son's natural aptitude without significant additional support. She is brilliant at critical thinking and generating and expressing divergent creative ideas, which is something my son has to work hard at achieving as he is more formulaic and literal in his thoughts and expression. The education system needs to ensure it accommodates these different learning styles. For this and many other valid reasons, there is an individualistic bias in how we are taught and assessed.

With some exceptions such as business school where there is a more team-based aspect to learning and application, for those who go onto higher education, this individualistic lens continues. When we get to the workplace, a continued individualistic paradigm through which we introduce, onboard, evaluate, assess and performance manage individuals in their professions is dominant. This often extends towards reward and pay and, in many functional areas, is responsible for revenue-generating activity. This leads to direct incentivisation of individuals' contributions or performance. Although at one level measurement is necessary, attributing individual performance can be detrimental to encouraging the more realistic social construct required for people to be productive in the workplace. Worst-case scenario, measurements using a mechanistic stance can trigger unhelpful constructs for individuals, which are then reinforced by inner traumas they experienced in other contexts even when unintended or unrelated.

I often have conversations with leaders and their teams that uncover unfounded narratives that covertly exist in their relationships with one another. With gentle facilitation, conversations that were not conducted previously reveal that a team member has held a protracted narrative of not being good enough or not performing their role in line with what they believed was expected of them. When their manager hears this, they dismantle the construct with specific evidence to the contrary. As their relationship develops, they learn that the construct may have been projected onto the manager in the absence of sufficient dialogue and shared connection. I see these situations frequently where previous relationship dynamics are brought into a current relationship and, without noticing or questioning this applied construct, interactions lack trust or appreciation and are instead infused with suspicion and speculation.

We will cover more on some of these dynamics from a systemic and cultural perspective in Chapters 6 and 7.

How organisations measure performance

Rooted in Frederick Taylor's teachings to the business world, measurement systems aimed at driving productivity and efficiency through utilisation of resources can also re-enforce this individualistic paradigm and lead to misleading or unhelpful measures. Coupled with a valid need that organisations have for certainty and control, measures informed by task-focused paradigms can even drive damaging outcomes. Jerry Muller, who wrote *The Tyranny of Metrics,* says: 'The costs of measuring may be greater than the benefits.

The things that get measured may draw effort away from the things we really care about.'[33]

FROM GREAT TO BRILLIANT

A business leader reached out to me about a team that had worked together for twelve years. Each of the team leaders heads up a region working in field operations. They are a high-performing team and agreed that they had already gone from good to great. They said they wanted 'to go from being a great team to becoming simply brilliant'. The business leader described his team leaders as rivalrous and focused on blame and regretted that they didn't support one another more. We live in a world where we must have each other's backs and look outwardly to succeed. To address their customer needs, they needed to find a way to leverage their capacities, capabilities and ability to learn and adapt across the different regions.

To use another swimming analogy, their leader had told them to stick to their individual lanes and let him be the one who surveyed the whole pool. The work I did with the team involved a 360 review for each individual so they could give each other feedback safely. I carried out a one-to-one conversation with each of them and then used the data to facilitate an honest conversational inquiry to learn in an appreciative way. During the journey I took with them, they transitioned from starting conditions centred around rivalry and competition into a solid, supportive team delivering even higher levels of performance and becoming role models for their neighbouring functions. This was during a turbulent period for the organisation because they were going through a major merger and were on the frontline of providing emergency services to consumers during the pandemic.

A proud moment that stood out for me was when, at the end of the first session after I asked for some reflections, one leader said that they were feeling extremely embarrassed but in equal measure thrilled about the fact that, although the team had known each other for over ten years, it only took one day with me for them to truly know each other. They had been out to the pub and music gigs and done lots of activities together, but they said they knew nothing about their colleagues compared to what they learned about them that day. Most of all, they experienced a sense of care for one another for the first time. Three months later, when the work was complete, they fed back to me that they now had each other's backs.

One goal of our work was to change the measurement process because they measured individual regions using a scoreboard, which led to competitive undercurrents and blame. We transitioned to individual measures as well as collective measures of success. It shifted entirely so that when one region wasn't performing as well, the other regions asked what they could do to support its performance rather than shaming them for being at the bottom of the list.

Do, do, do – deliver

Driven by our growing ambition and pace of development aimed at satisfying shareholder expectations, there is a relentless *task focus* within organisations that push for action and delivery at any cost.

A good example is the expectation of many leaders I work with who initially ask what the 'outputs' of a team session will be, the black and white 'next steps' required to justify the time investment by the team members or leaders away from their day-to-day activity. I love seeing the shift in leaders after a day of high-quality conversations with their teams – making meaningful connections and doing deep, constructive thinking together. The change manifests in how they operate, behave, think and interact, leading to impactful, desired outcomes.

A 'chicken and egg' dynamic exists with measurements implemented and upheld to drive 'aspired' performance and action. This never-ending bias towards doing, delivering and completing prevents us from stopping to question whether we are doing the right things. The vicious cycle of annual, quarterly, monthly and weekly planning and reporting drives behaviours more focused on the planning and doing than on the 'thinking' that is needed to diagnose, consider, connect with others, generate, ideate, review and iterate. Instead, the adrenaline buzz and illusion of 'doing' drives people to keep going and gives a delusional sense that nonstop activity leads to high-quality, meaningful results.

Despite positive intent, relatively modern commonplace methodologies like 'Agile' and 'Design Thinking' are introduced and become a loose part of the corporate language aimed at remaining competitive and driving 'order of magnitude' improvements. However, I see a lot of passionate people expending significant effort within the entrenched siloed paradigms and traditional top-down structures that may have once been appropriate but now lead to short-term, shifting, competing and conflicting priorities demanded by diverse stakeholders and trying to get the job done.

Management attention – leadership's core constraint

Just before he passed away, Eli Goldratt shared a view that management attention is the ultimate constraint in any organisation.[34] He suggested that there are more things that management could do to improve the business than they have the capacity for. So, the rate of ongoing improvement in an organisation is determined by this precious but finite capacity.

Despite a genuine desire to work collectively on shared goals, given the pace, growing expectations and need to demonstrate delivery, in most teams I work with, leaders and teams are inevitably forced to focus on their own functional territories and silos. Stepping back to look at the bigger picture is not intuitively considered a value-adding activity.

Zoom out and see more clearly together

Paradoxically, when a leadership team allows the time to stop and envision their journey, determine the best route and check they are clear on as many variables as possible *before* departing, it becomes much easier to focus on the few things that maximise their chances of reaching their destination on time and safely.

Working in individual functions, silos and even at a cross-functional level but with individual motivations drives local optimisation, meaning that progress and performance in one part of the business can have a detrimental effect on another part if they are not synchronised or timed appropriately.

In the health context, I have seen parts of the system run well when incentivised and perform beautifully in their own silo. I supported a hospital team to improve patient flow to enhance their capacity under growing demand. We reviewed all the steps in the patient's journey from surgery to getting physiotherapy or support after a hip replacement to getting ready to be discharged from a ward. Efficiency was driven hard in various disciplines. The occupational therapists (positioned towards the end of the patients' journeys) faced tremendous pressure as they had difficulties arranging the in-home equipment installations required for patients to take a bath. This was due to a policy put in place several years earlier requiring that they purchase from only one preferred supplier known to the chief executive at the time. This created a growing backlog that clogged up beds at the tail end of the patients' journeys. We made a vast improvement when the multidisciplinary team prioritised lobbying to contract with several new external suppliers of the equipment to fulfil the demand.

Good performance in a specific functional area does not guarantee results at a systemic level. An example of this is rapid growth in sales but an inadequate ability to satisfy customer demand, whether through insufficient stock or warehouse space, which may ultimately lead to lost sales and undermine brand value and customer loyalty. Objectives achieved at a functional level are not always fully leveraged on a cross-functional scale.

You come to me

Organisational barriers to generating time and space

It is difficult for leaders navigating today's volatile environment to create the time and the conditions needed to generate shared visibility – to simultaneously grasp and hold onto the bigger picture, the system, what individuals contribute and how this works interdependently with what their colleagues do. Generating this visibility requires trust – trust in leaders' intent and trust in team members – and a curiosity to better understand existing social relations for co-operation and collaboration to prevail. This can be extended and applied in a cross-functional context.

The pursuit of performance and delivery within the silos magnifies the need for trust and assumed good intent. Often, I see the opposite – people within a team avoiding a perceived risk or a functional domain impeding them from reaching out to others. To view the bigger picture holistically and gain a shared understanding, the team, stakeholders and leaders need to operate in a way that enables them to connect – connect on context, connect on shared goals, connect on each other's contributions, and ultimately connect on which individual choices that need to be made are synergistic and which are not. The divisional nature of how businesses are run and operate stems from the legitimate reductionist tendencies in a world where predictability was relatively more likely but in today's world is increasingly not the case.

When leaders come to me for support to help them individually or to help make their teams more effective, the undesirable realities they express are consistent connotations of the following:

- It's people issues that keep me awake at night.

- There is a lack of trust in my team (or between my team and other teams).

- I feel drained by the emotional stuff I encounter.

- I don't know how to help my people step up.

- I hire different people who are talented and they don't see eye to eye, so they disagree or fight, compete and backstab.

- Stakeholders on whom we are dependent have their own ideas about what we should do and how we should do it, but we struggle to solve the friction.

- It's 'us' versus 'them' all the time, not 'we'.

- My team delivers, but many people look tired, disengaged and burnt out.

- My team members compete for my attention and recognition.

I then ask them to look back on their week guided by two questions I learned from a mentor:

1. What are you doing that you feel you shouldn't be doing?

2. What do you believe you should be doing that you are not doing?

Without fail, the size of the first list is endless – a long, incoherent list of tasks.

List 2 typically includes:

- Time to pause, reflect and notice how I or we feel.

- Time to see the bigger picture that I or we need to consider.

- Time to have conversations with people that are unrelated to specific tasks.

- Time to think and co-create a view of the problems we face together and develop ways forward.

This sparks the realisation that the opportunities are scarce for shared and collective seeing, feeling and thinking about the bigger picture that the team inhabits and the social interactions they need to find shared clarity about their context and each other.

The opportunity mindfulness presents

Meditation is a discipline recognised as a powerful modality for training the mind to focus and redirect attention. It is becoming a mighty force for leaders and teams in this space. Chapter 4 described the benefits associated with managing stress, anxiety and depression. Recent studies indicate how, at a physiological level, mindful practice can affect neural pathways, reverse abnormalities relating to mental health and even lead to structural changes in the brain.[35] To top these compelling developments, mindfulness practices are now also being used in the context of teams. Meditation is showing promising evidence of impacting attention span, creativity and memory.[36]

Megan Reitz and Michael Chaskalson have been researching the effects of the practice of meditation and mindfulness by leaders and, more recently, the propensity of teams to navigate complex times, be more resilient and engender better collaboration. Insights gathered as part of an early eight-week study involving senior leaders (of which I was one) indicated that those who practised meditation (as little as ten minutes daily) experienced improved adaptability and the capacity for more perspective, focus, emotional regulation and empathy. 'When some combination of metacognition, curiosity and the process of allowing are present, a small "space" opens in the flow of experience where choiceful response becomes possible and reactivity is reduced.'[37]

Over the last decade, I have included meditation in my one-to-one and team coaching activities. This is not a straightforward sell; I often find myself needing to explain and justify the value of using breathwork to ground and create a calm and open space to slow down from the busy pace of organisational life. After individuals with little or no experience of mindful exercise try it out, many share that discomfort and awkwardness emanate from internal voices in their heads. I encourage further experimentation and perseverance, treating mindful activity like the formation of a new experience and eventually a habit. A resource I use and refer clients to is the Calm app and I strongly recommend Megan Reitz's Mindful Leadership Meditations.

In Chapter 4, we explored the notion of creating mindful spaces to generate conditions for deepening self-awareness and how a deliberate effort is needed to interrupt our busy lives. In the context of teams, the need for this space is equally important. A contemporary movement is gradually taking effect in which coaches (and other practitioners) are designing 'retreats' for leaders and people to purposefully create and inhabit this space for mindful work in the company of peers in a conducive, natural environment. A small step I ask leaders to take is to incorporate 'walk and talks' with colleagues into their work weeks. A suggestion is to find a way to walk outdoors, ideally in natural surroundings.

Coming back to the physics principle of 'refraction', light refracts as it travels between different mediums distinguished by high or low densities. Light speeds up when travelling from a high-density medium like water to a low-density medium like air, and the reverse is true. Refraction offers a frame for busy teams ineffectively multi-tasking their way through a muddled and opaque journey. Refracting permits a shared vantage point by stopping, stepping back, breathing in, considering each other and getting a whole feel for the bigger picture with greater collective perspective. As light enters a new medium, the angle at which it refracts enhances the team's visibility and generates new angles and possibilities.

Bedding down

Darshan's swimming story is a relevant representation of a team whose bigger picture is clear – they want to win and be the best swim team they can be. Individually, swimmers know it isn't as simple as each swimmer striving to be the best, even though their individual performance and improvements are critical. What strikes me is that their coach drives each of them technically, which was something I noticed as Darshan developed his swimming skills in earlier years, and some emphasis on this continues to be relevant.

There are subtle techniques that help build skill and impact performance. Watching the swimmers during training sessions and galas, it is amazing to notice the conversations they have in small groups, across all ages and genders. They often comment on each other's performance, how well they did, how hard they see others pushing themselves, and sometimes encourage each other with tips for better dives, strokes and tumble turns. Most of the time, they connect and check out how they are doing outside the pool and in their day-to-day lives. Darshan craves the moment his swim practice arrives each day, even on Fridays at 5.45am. He loves improving; he loves exceeding his targets (which he does regularly because he works hard) but, most of all, he loves being part of the team and is determined to help the team meet its goal.

In Chapter 6, we will look at the power of a systemic view, contrasting this with some of the more classic perspectives we use to understand what happens in organisations. We will also explore some challenges that make connecting with others in organisations complex and may even drive avoidance.

A SPACE FOR YOU TO REFRACT

1. How would you describe the quality of connection with your colleagues?

2. What gets in the way of you cultivating more meaningful connections?

3. To what extent do you feel you share a common view of the bigger picture with your team and relevant stakeholders? What are the consequences of this?

4. How often do you get out and spend time in natural surroundings as part of your weekly life?

5. How does the concept of meditation land for you? What would make you more open to or curious about its benefit?

6. If meditation is already a practice of yours, what might motivate you to ensure it features even more in your routines?

6
Seeing The System

Beaming a light to awaken you...

Systems do not exist without selves. Understanding your integral role within any system you inhabit is the crucial key to unlocking and enjoying the benefits that the system has to offer you and those you share it with.

Pivoting back to my 'self'

The abrupt detour my family was forced to take in 2017 hit us hard. The changes I faced in getting my family back on track were even tougher. Getting back to 'normal' involved refreshing the aura of our home from the stale and static energy and scent of illness that had inhabited the house during the preceding months. We had travelled to and from hospitals and had various family members and friends staying over to support us. Though severely depleted in energy and motivation, I knew it was time to recreate our home.

This time also involved guiding Anees, my seven-year-old daughter, back to a place of feeling safe and loved, and helping her make sense of the shadow under which she had lived for the duration of her brother's illness and treatment. Often smiling and disseminating an energy that provided respite after the darkness, in the outside world, Anees appeared to be a symbol of relief and comfort to those witnessing our integration back into life. Seeing her veneer of quiet composure at school and a young but wise determination, her teachers would tell us how impressed they were by her ability to bounce back from the interruptions to her second year in primary school. This outward show was in bleak contrast to the anger and resentment spilling out in the privacy of our home. Countless nights involved tearful explosions of fear, resentment and anger during which she desperately needed calm, nurturing conditions and my unconditional presence following the abandonment she experienced.

This phase also required me to help Darshan reintegrate socially when his peers had developed their friendships in his absence through video gaming, developed athletically and continued their childhoods while he was in and out of the hospital. During this challenging transition, I worked closely with Darshan to determine where he would go to senior school. This resulted in a dilemma about whether it would be better to encourage his preparation for a challenging eleven-plus exam which, if he passed, would grant him acceptance to a grammar school or let him take it slowly and not succumb to the pressure that the entrance exam would entail.

It involved supporting my husband, Fraser, to return to his own professional life: to enter a corporate setting in which he was able to perform and make up for the time he took off to support our son. Fraser took on triathlon training and competition, a source of escape that provided a therapeutic space in which he could heal at his own pace. He would ride his bike for hours, take swimming lessons and run to alleviate the pain and recognition of the unwanted path he had travelled.

These and many more needs, such as the emotional intensity of dealing with frequent scans and tests to provide reassurance that the cancer was permanently gone, consumed us. The family needed my focus to recreate our life, which meant that there was no time available for me to recover and recalibrate as a woman, mother, wife and professional. It took at least a year and a half for me to carve out the time to start focusing on my own needs. When it finally became possible to allow some free time for myself, I experienced several physiological symptoms, including skin ailments, acute pain and digestive challenges. I cocooned into a shell and began to notice I was struggling with social connections and the ability to nurture friendships. I suffered a paralysing lack of self-esteem, which fuelled a dissociation from my professional identity and I feared the loss of all my abilities.

Two years later, I began my studies in biomedicine with a view to better understanding naturopathy and nutrition. By then, I had stepped back into my coaching work. One session at a time, I reminded myself of my vocation, the power of my work, the impact it had on others and how capable and skilled I am in what I do as a coach and organisational consultant. After noticing frequent episodes of strong emotional surges, chest palpitations and depressive feelings, I started working with a psychotherapist. These signs led me to realise that I needed to process my journey during and after the traumatic period I had endured. And then the COVID pandemic hit...

An opportunity arose to work as an executive coach for leaders and teams within a large corporate organisation during their multifaceted transformation. I secured the role as a leadership coach contracted to create and launch a coaching-based leadership development scheme for senior leaders and teams. I threw myself back into the rhythm of full-time work, becoming one of fourteen thousand employees and a leadership coach, facilitator and advisor in a business going through a historical joint venture and digital transformation. The following twenty months were a hothouse of learning and embodied experience of operating within *the system*. Having spent so many years working as a consultant within a business school and start-ups followed by self-employment, I had not experienced being inside a corporate organisation. It was a fascinating experience and, although after completing the position my preference was to resume my independent role and remain outside the system, it provided invaluable insights into and deep intuitive embodied experience of how I can help my clients in an even more meaningful way.

Lenses through which we see organisations

When I reflect on the management theory surrounding organisational behaviour, I go back to one set of lenses through which organisations can be viewed and understood. Gareth Morgan, who wrote *Images of Organization,* paints a wide variety of metaphors from mechanistic to humanistic with representations such as machine, organism, brain, culture, political systems, flux and transformation.[38] He offers a way to better understand and analyse how businesses operate and behave, and his emphasis is on how this behaviour helps them to solve problems.

Over the years, I have seen two core frames or paradigms used within organisations and their leadership as levers for performance, desired outcomes or to influence wanted changes. The first is the 'hard', more tangible and technical frame – rooted in the machine metaphor, with origins in scientific theory and Frederick Taylor's view of organisational improvement and change as a product of our focus on structures, processes, management systems and other technical capabilities.

Scientific theory in the industrial era governed how we saw the world and solved problems using a reductionist approach – breaking things down into parts and solving each individually. In most client organisations in which I work, the dominant reality is a need to separate functions, run each part as a division and develop a collection of individual operating models that change iteratively and frequently to optimise local performance. It is a way of understanding and seeing the world – the quest to get to the nub of cause and effect and find a solution that grants results.

In my experience, this approach is helpful to enhance our understanding of parts and get a sense of measures. There is value in this perspective, which brings about clarity and focus. But it is challenging to keep tabs on the environment and certain dependencies that are fluid and simply out of our control – therefore it can undermine outcomes in the absence of guarantees driven by complexity. Also, using only this lens relies on linear correlations or causes and effects and makes it challenging to notice patterns.

An alternative frame is a more humanistic view, underpinned by the psychological and sociological theories we explored in Chapter 5, that sees organisations through the lens of their people.

Do you see what I see?

A systemic view

Systems theory is a field of inquiry and application in which language and concepts around transformation and ecosystems are emerging. In this context, systems are not defined as the more technical, tangible systems that organisations invest in such as IT. Rather, as summarised by Joan Lurie, a leading authority in systemic change, they are 'the complex web and patterns of interrelating between the members or parts of the organisation system and the roles that they play'.[39]

The predecessor of this theoretical basis is the complex adaptive systems perspective or complexity theory pioneered by Ralph Stacey, a British organisational theorist.[40] This sits more closely with Morgan's metaphors of the organism and the network. We are increasingly seeing more references to ecosystems and the interconnected nature of this frame in organisations and in relation to digital transformations.

In addition to seeing organisations as collections of people and processes, this more ecological lens helps us to see organisations as an interdependent web. This includes tangible entities like technology, facilities, buildings, the environment and people and less tangible elements like culture, informal communication, tacit knowledge, discretionary effort and 'how things get done around here'. It is vital to pay attention to the complex sets of interrelated interactions that exist and morph.

The roots of dependency in human relations

In a human or mammalian context, the 'basic assumption of dependency' states that, because babies are born helpless, the concept of dependency exists and is a pre-requisite for life. Interdependency is fundamental to the function of a human system, its ability to operate and be generative. Organisational behaviour is not just an effect of people and their relationships, it is also an effect of the interdependent nature of the various entities that form part of the organisation. Interdependency can exist between entities like people, teams, subsets and hierarchical structures of the organisation. They also co-exist in context with goals and measures and correspond to the external world in relationships with customers and stakeholders.

A critical and often overlooked aspect is the role for which each of these entities is recruited and contracted to play. Systemic thinkers like Joan Lurie and Simon Western enlighten us about the 'relatedness' between the roles people are given (eg the application of a job title when a person is hired) and how this becomes a symbol of power within the system with the potential to imprint on and influence their perceived value in the organisation.[41] The same can apply to what Western refers to as nonhuman entities or 'objects' like a client relationship, a subscription or brand. These 'objects' also become entities that interrelate with the wider environment and influence the culture and values that are generated and develop over time.[42]

Defining power

It is helpful to note some definitions of terms relating to power when considering the interrelationships that exist in a system. A classic view stems from Thomas Hobbes, a political philosopher, who helped us to understand power as the ability to exercise control over another person and impose the need for obedience. Known for his interest in how humans could find harmony and avoid conflict in societal life, he defined the following terms:[43]

- **Domination** is the ability to force your will upon another and get them to do something they would not otherwise choose to do.

- **Authority** is the right to make others comply.

- **Legitimacy** is the perception that power is exercised rightfully.

- **Influence** is the ability to affect an outcome even in the absence of the power to decide.

Although our understanding of the nuances relating to power has evolved, my experience is that some of these foundational interpretations still hold true in many corporate organisational contexts.

A relationship between power and dependency

According to Emerson (1962), the basis of power is dependency.[44] A depends on B if A has goals and needs that B can fulfil. For example, an employee depends on their employer for financial security in the form of a salary. Similarly, an employer depends on its employees for labour, capability and capacity.

The gift of systemic thinking is that it offers the ability to see patterns. Patterns enable us to see ourselves as part of the system rather than judging it. A systems lens helps people to see the bigger picture with some level of detachment without going so far that they separate themselves from the interactions within it. This introduces the potential to reframe ourselves and others within those patterns, which can liberate us to rethink our relationship with the system.

Systems thinking can also be challenging because thinking systemically takes away the capacity for us to attribute blame. Allocating responsibility is not possible, as the whole system generates a mesh of interconnected conditions that contribute to the undesirable effects experienced. Although there may be a potential cause of the problem, the complexity of human, emotional, energetic and relational attributes makes it impossible to address it without truly understanding the interrelatedness of the entities. The outcome of the system is an effect of various interactions – not one specific point in the system.

The common tendency for many leaders is to perceive themselves as being separate from the system. Language suggesting *me versus the system* or *us versus them* tends to be used generically, making it easier to attribute blame elsewhere if things are not working in line with expectations. This leads to generalisations that do not help people understand or commit to specifically what is not working and needs to change. Importantly, this prevents an opportunity for a leader to acknowledge their own (or their team members') role in contributing to the changes that are needed and creates a situation where the leader can disassociate themselves and their team from the problem.

The systemic approach creates a different type of interaction and relationship, which is inclusive of all people and the system they inhabit. This stops people from looking at a system and analysing, judging or diagnosing it from a distance and taking no responsibility and action. This approach leaves no space to blame or point fingers but encourages collective action and responsibility instead. A systemic approach requires individuals, groups of people and teams to self-examine, embrace what feels uncomfortable and explore the implications of conflicts using a lens that studies the whole picture with positive intent and curiosity, avoiding any notion of blame.

Keeping the blame moving.

The significance of an individual's role and contract in a system

A systemic and ecological view of organisations offers a perspective I increasingly apply in my work with organisations, teams and individuals. The nuanced and interconnected components that make up what happens in organisations are easy to overlook. When there is a perceived problem, I hear a lot of blame or speculation aimed at a person's or a group's behaviour, approach and capabilities or lack thereof. This may be true to some degree, however, if we switch paradigms and understand behaviour using a systemic lens, we start to understand our problems differently and our solutions and interventions to address them are also quite different.

I feel like I'm just their tennis ball

Joan Lurie talks in her conversation with Simon Western about how, in a system, it is critical to find the patterns in interactions between people who are contracted to perform specific roles with expectations in terms of contribution, capabilities, experience and status. She defines the term 'relatedness' as different to relationships.[45]

The roles that people occupy in different contexts in organisations at different times drive diverse sets of complex behaviours. Typically, people don't simply get one job that remains rigid and static when they join an organisation despite most classically being labelled with one job title. In today's fluid and rapidly changing work environment, people play multiple roles each day. This is different from the classical frames we subscribed to in what may have been a more predictable world in businesses of the past.

On any given day during my time as an employee in a corporate organisation, I worked as an executive coach to a senior director, a mentor to a graduate, a facilitator to one of the leadership teams, the head of our coaching faculty, a team leader of a cross-functional team, an advisor to one of its C-suite executives, a peer to a colleague, a subordinate to my manager and a tutor on a training programme. This means I was an employee in a wide organisational ecology of diverse roles. How we behave based on our roles leads to a complex set of emotional, rational and embodied experiences.

After over twenty years as an external consultant to businesses cultivating consultant-client relationships built on legitimate authority, I was suddenly subordinate to an HR professional. I frequently felt misunderstood and at times coerced to play roles that were at odds with my understanding of the needs of teams and the organisation. The approaches they asked me to come up with were fundamentally at odds with the wisdom of my intuition. Given my perspective and awareness, I had the capability to review the 'contracts' with each stakeholder/stakeholder group with whom I needed to establish a working relationship. This sometimes seemed messy and intruded on my sense of self-worth, but I managed these shifts in roles by evaluating what role I was playing and for what purpose in each context and explicitly checking in with relevant stakeholders.

Zooming out further, I was also able to broaden the perspective I held about the wider system encompassing my relationship to the corporate organisation at that point in my life and profession, and to revisit my intent in joining it given the requirements I needed to satisfy. The clarity this wider context offered me broadened my array of choices about how to address the limitations relating to my ability to contribute in line with my potential, and establish whether further personal growth was possible within the organisation.

Relational lens

Life is relational. The philosopher Martin Heidegger identified 'being-in-the-world' as one of life's core existential truths.[46] Over the years, I have honed and finessed how I use the term 'relational' in my work with clients, based on my schooling in this field from people like Bill Critchley, Charlotte Sills, Erik de Haan and Simon Cavicchia. I understand this concept to mean being mindful of the symbiotic nature of the social process two or more people share at any point in time and throughout their relationship, placing importance on creating conditions for co-authoring, co-crafting, co-creating in the moment, and for this to be a generative basis of shared learning, change and transformation.

Learning to see our organisations systemically, viewing the system as a whole and noticing the roles we play across those systems enable us to be more conscious, resourceful, choiceful and skilful at switching between the multiple roles organisations need us to play to make the relevant contributions in line with rapidly shifting needs – in a way that is relational.

A need to be held

It was early in the pandemic when I joined the corporate organisation. I was approached for a senior role at a consultancy and it triggered the idea that, as a pandemic was on its way, it might be a good move for me to join an organisation. I felt lonely and vulnerable at the time and had just started sessions with the psychotherapist I mentioned earlier because I was questioning myself in so many ways following my son's illness and having lost connection with my identity as a successful professional.

The disruption to my life had been significant, and the self-doubt and worry about whether I was ever going to get back to where I had been terrified me. I was also experiencing unexpected symptoms in my body. I had an itchy rash all over my chest and underarms, which woke me up every night. The rash was ugly with red dots, and I didn't understand what it was or what caused it. My hair became stringy and fell out in clumps. I also suffered excruciating neck pain. I grew anxious and fearful that something was wrong with me. This prompted me to start seeing an integrative therapist (a functional medicine expert). I was studying biomedicine at the College of Naturopathic Medicine and was aware I could support my health in various ways that would help me through this unsettling time.

I joined the corporate organisation thinking how comforting it would be to have someone take care of me for a change. After being self-employed for so many years, the thought of being in an organisation with attractive benefits was alluring, especially given the unravelling uncertainty that accompanied the COVID announcements. I was consoled when my therapist said that maybe it was my turn to be held. I realised that it is OK to be helped.

During that time, I also became conscious through a few conversations that I was angry, furious even – not about what had happened but about the fact that, after having spent years reaching out, supporting and consulting peers and providing people with work opportunities, it felt like no one did that for me when I needed it most. Given some of my clients were incredibly understanding when my son was ill and told me to invoice them and do the work when I was able, it embarrassed me to ask them for more work later. I felt a sort of shame and lacked the confidence to ask anyone for help. I grew resentful, which became apparent in my work with my therapist.

So, I joined this organisation to be supported, to be given employee benefits, to be part of a team and to have social connection during the pandemic. Functionally, the role made absolute sense. I was a leadership coach working for the organisation and the work was fantastic. I was hired to set up a programme for the senior leaders of the organisation, which didn't take me long. Most importantly, I was also coaching, which was the piece that really tapped into my '*iki-gai*' (the Japanese concept of 'reason for being' that combines passion, capability, mission, vocation and profession).[47] Before I knew it, I was doing a lot of coaching with leadership teams across the business and the work I did was in great demand because the organisation was undergoing an unprecedented virtual transformation.

Lucky enough to take my Ikigai to work

Bedding down

Looking back at the power dynamics I faced during my time in a corporate system, I am grateful for what I learned. On reflection, when I entered as a subject matter expert who worked with the senior leaders, having a role that was hierarchy-agnostic was problematic.

Because of the role and my position within the business, the division within which I was hired and its hierarchical culture, there were times when I wasn't invited to strategy communications events with the most senior leaders even though I was their coach. I led a faculty of highly skilled executive coaches who relied on me to be aware of the strategic context but in the formal hierarchical structure I was not classified as a Director, void of the privileges needed to be invited to key events, making it impossible for me to fulfil aspects of my job. Having previously worked with senior leaders and C-suite directors in organisations in which I had access to strategic content, it was strange. I felt like I was in the dark. Admittedly the situation changed quickly because I had influence with stakeholders who then allowed me to attend the meetings, but it was troubling that it had occurred.

One of the most interesting outcomes of that time was that I noticed some of the less conscious and visible dynamics in the power plays between me and parts of the system (whether individuals, teams or levels within the system). It brought to life some of the complexities driven by my dependence on the organisation. I noticed my dependency on earning, being respected, being considered authoritative and having legitimacy after twenty-five years in my field.

I noticed an unconscious dynamic between me and a leader in a position of power: our dependency became mutual for a short period. I brought expertise, skills and capacity to enable this person to view the system and understand which aspects they had to address. This involved some difficult dilemmas and meant they became dependent on some of the interventions I led. I became equally dependent on them, not only for the legitimacy by association that I felt I needed for my work but also for my confidence. It took a couple of months for me to realise that a subconscious dynamic resulted from this dependency. I now know just how instrumental that insight was.

This relationship triggered several of my drivers: to be admired for my hard work and capability, to be accepted by someone I respected (almost revered) for their intellect and to be acknowledged for my worth by someone powerful. I was motivated to invest disproportionate efforts well beyond the scope of my role. I don't believe there was any ill intent on their part, but it does make me reflect on the power play and my role inside and outside of this system. I am pleased I was able to spot and withdraw from the situation and I learned an enormous amount about myself and the organisation.

In the next chapter, we will explore the complexities that stem from cultural differences and their importance in an organisational context.

A SPACE FOR YOU TO REFRACT

1. Does the concept of dependency resonate for you? How might it show up in your life?

2. How might a systemic lens enable you to understand the world you inhabit better?

3. What power dynamics have you navigated in your life?

4. When you reflect on these situations, what personal needs influenced and were impacted by these dynamics?

5. How is being more mindful of this helpful to you?

6. What is the significance of the role and job title you hold?

7
Valuing Difference

Beaming a light to awaken you…

Truly and respectfully valuing difference is as important as taking personal responsibility for our responses to the behaviours we see others exhibit towards us.

Standing out *and* fitting in

The tapestry of my life is enriched by the cultural differences I traverse as part of such a large, diverse and complex family.

I am grateful for the myriad of childhood experiences to which I was exposed, including time in faraway lands like Karachi where I spent long summers with my Indian and Pakistani families.

Memories of the goat herder calling out 'Bakri, Bakri!' in the mornings, as he roamed the narrow alley where my paternal grandfather Abba lived, still linger with me. I remember looking out of my window and seeing twenty or more goats taking their final fateful walk before being served up for that evening's supper and unsuccessfully begging my dad to have one as my pet instead. I cherish memories of the markets: the colour, the chaos and the mixture of sounds as shop tellers persistently followed us to barter as we roamed the market stalls. The smells so intensely infused with spices, body odours and animal meat are unforgettable. Our family gatherings involved just sitting together. Often in silence, we would look at each other with curtains drawn to keep out the sweltering heat – I recall a sense of calm, quiet connection and raw and obscure intimacy.

Being with my father's side, whether in Pakistan, India or Australia, was such a contrast to the rambunctious and gregarious barbecue get-togethers in my maternal Venezuelan habitat. Every year our 120-plus strong community of cousins would hold a family event right after Christmas to honour our parents, aunts and uncles – the elders of the family. The events involved tumultuous exchanges of humour: lots of laughter, teasing and storytelling with abrupt interruptions and meandering tangents. There was colourful food made from homegrown produce like enormous avocados and papayas. The parties would involve loud music, dancing, children riding toy motorcycles and open forms of affection like hugging, kissing and holding each other. Energy activates every cell in my body as I reminisce.

The cross-fertilisation of my experience is rooted in a world well-travelled and where, existentially, my intrinsic feelings about humanity are a messy, bound-aryless mishmash of cultural fusion and antithesis. Moving to the UK when I was fourteen, studying, working, eventually marrying a British man and identifying as partly British has been a provocative journey for me. I am appreciative of, grateful for and allegiant to the country and culture that have offered me a safe home, love and opportunities for stabil-ity and growth. My ascension as a young adult and professional was coated with British strokes of polite reserve, self-control and rule-driven conformity. Although, as an immigrant, there are times when I find myself responding with resistance to established cultural norms that I find different to the status quo, I have inexorably adopted some of these as my own.

Growing into adulthood and living in the UK, I have seen and felt uncomfortable tensions in cultural differences come to life. Becoming a mother led to experiences of uneasy distinctions and this fuelled the unhelpful narrative I harboured from my childhood around feeling self-doubt, too different or not good enough. There is one situation that particularly stands out and has manifested tensions that have coloured some family dynamics. Two months after Darshan was born, we were invited to a family Christmas gath-ering. Within moments of arriving, I was asked to breastfeed Darshan in the back room or somewhere away from those present. I was told it was to spare others the embarrassment of me exposing myself as I breastfed. I was shocked, given the discreet way in which I fed my baby and how natural and important I consider breastfeeding for the nourishment and emotional development of an infant.

Rather than questioning what I simply interpreted as a norm or causing any unpleasantness, I masked my response (as did my husband Fraser) and I did as I was asked. I breastfed Darshan on several occasions each day, which is usual for a young baby, and these feeds took quite some time. This translated to significant periods during which I sat in a separate room with my baby and a book. Despite the quality bonding time with my son, I felt alienated from the family because I already spent considerable solitary time with Darshan at all hours of the day and night when I was at home. It also created a situation that Fraser found hard. Finding a balance between spending time with us and the wider family left him torn. Such is the power of conflict underpinned by cultural difference.

What is culture and why is it important?

According to PwC's *2021 Global Culture Survey* of 3,200 leaders and employees, organisational culture is a topic of growing importance on leadership agendas.[48] In 2013, 53% of respondents considered it a priority and this increased to 67% at the time of the survey. 72% of leaders and employees claim that culture supports successful change initiatives. 69% of senior leaders credit much of their success during the pandemic to their approach to culture. During a year that necessitated major changes for companies around the world, over two-thirds of respondents said that their culture helped their change initiatives. Similarly, almost 70% of those who said their organisations were able to adapt over the previous year also reported that their organisation's culture was a source of competitive advantage.

National culture is generated by a group of people, raised in a particular country, who have similar experiences and views on how things should be done, underpinned by shared values typically formed early in life. National culture becomes apparent in a critical mass of people and manifests in generic characteristics. The smaller the group of people, the greater the likelihood of seeing individual personality traits rather than a culture.

Organisational culture, a concept brought to organisations from the fields of social psychology and anthropology in the 1980s by Edgar Schein from MIT, refers to how people within an organisation relate to one another, their function and the wider context (eg shareholders, competitors and customers). An organisational or corporate culture can become more noticeable when compared with other organisational cultures. Culture is also influenced by the clarity of the business's vision, goal, purpose and objectives; how these translate into working practices, processes and policies; and how relatable or recognisable all of this is to its people. The extent to which a culture supports these elements can be strongly influential in the success of bringing its vision to fruition.

The iceberg

Schein introduced the popular metaphor and imagery outlining organisational culture as three layers of an iceberg:[49]

1. Artifacts and behaviours

2. Espoused values

3. Assumptions

This model highlights what is visible and what is not – what is relatively superficial, and what is not.

Artifacts are the tangible aspects that can be seen and touched. They include printed collateral with stated values and commitments, how people dress, job titles and physical office design. Despite a strong emphasis on artifacts because of their relative tangibility, businesses invest millions in broadcasting value statements using printed collateral with little or no tangible shift in culture and behaviour.

Espoused values are the organisation's rules of behaviour, principles and stipulations about how people should act when representing the organisation both internally and to its customers. These also include organisational charts, vision, purpose, mission statements and the printed communications that convey announcements.

I often work with organisations that are genuinely committed to their espoused values. Although their leadership encourages their people to adopt them, they cannot live by the values themselves because of systemic complexities and so they come across as disingenuous. It can confuse employees when expectations are stated in one way but reality suggests the opposite. These contradictions can affect individuals, subgroups and the whole organisation, generating unhealthy and unsettling dynamics, leading to a toxic environment with disgruntled people and passive-aggressive or cynical behaviours.

An organisation encouraging values like courage, honesty and collaboration, and whose strategic intent is to transform 70% of its customer services from a call centre to an AI-based digital platform, is likely to experience a backlash. Although it makes sense to encourage the leaders and people who are working hard to deliver this transformation, there is a human and personal cost to a transformation that will test the adoption of these values.

But it is the third layer of the iceberg – the deeper assumptions, invisible undercurrents which are less obvious and arguably more challenging to work with – that make the biggest difference to changing culture. People within the same organisation will have their own beliefs, values, assumptions, experiences and views of the company culture. How people are positioned across the hierarchical levels of the organisation has a significant influence on these perspectives, which are also coloured by those people's histories, psychological attachments and the shifting fabric of their lives.

Leaders hold their own beliefs; some of these are not directly verbalised but nevertheless influence those leaders' expectations. A good example is the 'return to the office' narrative when it became safe to be back in the workplace. The management of messaging and expectations has varied across industries and companies during different periods throughout the pandemic. The belief by segments of corporate employees that working from home is an appropriate replacement for office work continues to generate controversy. The leadership of some businesses may not have been sufficiently explicit about their underlying preference for getting people back into their high-cost rental offices. Others have been more prescriptive and expectant. A deeper set of values, assumptions and current day needs held by individual leaders and employees exists deep under the iceberg we encounter relating to a new era where home working, office working and a hybrid version all co-exist.

We all have different life stories, values and, therefore, perspectives so reconciling these differences is an important part of how I work with organisational cultures. Lately, I see more organisations and businesses recognising the significance of company culture, and there are many stories about businesses successfully harnessing it:

Examples of organisations whose culture is considered aspirational

Netflix: A culture of freedom and responsibility

Netflix is guided by the culture strategy outlined in its 127-page slide deck first made public in 2009, which has powered up conversations and interactions between employees.[50] Since its creation, it has become well known for inspiring the policies of HR departments around the world. In a famous update to the culture deck, its 2017 corporate manifesto on culture exuded the principle of prioritising 'people over process'.[51]

At the time of writing this book, Glassdoor reported that 87% of employees recommend working at Netflix. The secret sauce is perceived to be the company's ability to balance people's freedom with the sharing of responsibility for their behaviour and decision-making. Instead of an emphasis on artifacts and perks, Netflix says: 'Our version of the great workplace is not comprised of sushi lunches, great gyms, fancy offices or frequent parties. Our version of the great workplace is a dream team in pursuit of ambitious common goals.'

However, factors like stronger competition from other players as well as inflationary hikes affecting consumers are driving declines in revenue and market share. This compromises its long-standing admirable culture recipe with a steep and publicly exposed hike in layoffs.[52]

DHL: Embracing diversity through learning

DHL's emphasis is on leveraging its multicultural environment through learning and talent development and health and wellbeing. DHL built its cultural strategy around deeply held values of embracing diversity and promoting and creating learning possibilities for its people. In 2022, DHL ranked seventh in UK's Best Workplaces™ (Super Large, 1,000+ employees) and sixth in UK's Best Workplaces™ for Wellbeing. Great Place to Work's CEO Michael Bush stated:

> '92% of their people from the top of the organization to the frontline say it is a Great Place to Work For All. Their secret? Being purpose driven and having the most innovative and comprehensive "Certified International Specialist" training program in the world.'[53]

Zoom: Delivering happiness

'Truly delivering happiness for all employees' was a review posted on Glassdoor in January 2022. Zoom's mission is to 'develop a people-centric cloud service that transforms the real-time collaboration experience and improves the quality and effectiveness of communications forever'.[54] CEO Eric Yuan left Cisco WebEx because he was unhappy in his job. He was keen to understand what made customers happy and then he built a platform designed to deliver that product. Turbocharged by the requirement too for virtual connectivity for people, presented by the pandemic, this is how Zoom, the famous global brand, became a verb in our everyday vocabulary.

Zoom's market cap is $129 billion. Despite having to address enormous obstacles given privacy and security challenges, it grew exponentially. Employees describe their leaders as modelling the behaviours they encourage and being holistic in how they lead, which lacks a silo mentality.

Spotify: Small Swedish company culture

Despite paramount growth, Spotify has maintained Swedish business characteristics such as a flat management structure, selective recruitment criteria to avoid 'prima-donnas', a team ethos, transparency in decision-making and certain perks required by Swedish law, such as six months' maternity and parental leave for new parents.

Spotify was one of the first to adapt to pandemic-related societal changes by introducing a 'work from anywhere policy' for employees and, in 2021, employees could take a week off to recover from the stresses rooted in the pandemic. Cultural aspects like the concept of *fika*, a coffee break where informal and personal conversations are encouraged, continue to form a part of the rituals enjoyed by employees.

Ching-Wei Chen, the director of machine learning engineering said, 'Spotify is the biggest company

I have worked for, and it feels like the smallest. In terms of red tape and hierarchy, it feels like a small company.'

It is a business that has continued to grow, evolve and adapt and has happy employees. In 2021, the company was valued at $42 billion with revenues of $10 billion and humbly claims the secret to success is having nice people.

There is a growing list of organisations; some quite new in terms of their lifecycle and others more established, that recognise that culture needs to develop and support the strategic intent of the organisation – as well as take into account the social dimensions emerging in line with how our world evolves.

What do organisations that inspire you have in common?

1. What do you see as the main characteristics of these companies that are perceived to have admirable company cultures?

2. What do they do to support people?

3. How are organisational and business requirements also being nurtured and maintained?

4. Consider those organisations you come across that don't do well with their company culture. What are they doing or not doing?

The consequences of not paying attention to culture

Peter Drucker's famous quote about culture eating strategy for breakfast has echoed around the chambers of corporations for decades.

Unlike the more quantifiable challenges presented by inadequate financial health, the consequences of poor culture are less obvious and often hidden, but they eventually reveal themselves through unproductive employees, quiet quitting and toxic behaviours that undermine the value and reputation of the business.

Culture can be divisive and restrictive and lead to alienating behaviours. These might include blame, discrimination, bullying, grievances and attrition – all of which increase operating costs and diminish morale. This does not generate the conditions for an attractive place to work and it impacts recruitment potential. Although a healthy culture does not guarantee success, it remains a necessary condition for happy, productive employees, and a poor culture strongly enhances the chances of failure.

Yet, it is challenging to get it right, especially in well-established organisations whose cultures that have morphed along the way and that find it difficult to change.

FEAR OF BEING FIRED AGAIN

Chris was fired as the senior manager in an organisation many years before I met him. It was a familiar scenario of a new leader looking to start afresh. His dismissal was more reflective of the structural changes taking place in the organisation than his individual capabilities or contribution, but his sudden job loss shocked him. It felt like a personal attack on his self-esteem. The timing seemed even worse with a second child on the way. Although he quickly found a new job and continued to deliver successful results in a different organisation, the feelings of loss, self-doubt and fear lingered and weighed him down. The fear of losing his job again became a threat response regularly provoked by anything that challenged his sense of professional esteem and integrity, tainting his career experience.

During his early years in the new organisation, Chris worked for a leader with extremely high expectations. Although he could fulfil those expectations, his fear of not meeting them caused him to dread being fired again if he didn't always deliver. As a result, he experienced colossal levels of stress, which led to back pain and dermatological issues. It took him some time to realise that other team members felt similar levels of pressure and stress, and a culture lacking in psychological safety prevailed more widely.

The work we did together was designed to help him recognise how hooked he was into accommodating his boss's demands unconditionally, and how this was a damaging pattern. With my support, he explored his willingness to meet his boss's expectations, even at a disproportionate cost to his state of mind and physical wellbeing. Once he recognised his unconscious pattern, we worked out ways for him to assess the demands he faced to establish what was and wasn't appropriate.

He became more proactive in questioning the feedback he received and more confident about which criteria to use to judge requests and how much choice he had in whether to accommodate them. Over time his sense of authority grew, enabling him to challenge and shift the fear-based undercurrents disempowering members of the team by demonstrating and modelling changes in his behaviour.

Culture surveys

Organisations use workplace surveys and question-naires to gather data and attempt to translate insight into the appropriate areas of the business to enhance their culture. In the 1990s, when surveys became a hot tool for this purpose, clear correlations between operational performance and leadership behaviours emerged.

For example, the upstream procurement unit of an oil and gas business I worked with around twenty years ago suffered the consequences of poor supplier rela-tionships. A survey highlighted that poor employee satisfaction correlated with a command-and-control culture, which led to undesirable supplier relation-ships when 60% of the resources they depended on were outsourced at that time. The survey also showed that business units in which managers exercised a relatively high degree of control could not secure the services of suppliers in the same way as those with more autonomous staff. By encouraging changes in management style through learning and development and sourcing best practices, the cost of shifting towards win-win relationships with long-term suppliers reduced by 22%, avoiding the constant changes that had impacted reliability and availability.

Unfortunately, not all surveys produce such useful information; they can be misleading and a waste of time. Surveys aimed at assessing performance or leadership skills can be unhelpful and encourage speculation or subjective judgments of character traits. There is also the risk of insufficient sample sizes or a lack of comparative data. Careful and informed survey design helps maximise the relevance of the data.

'Survey fatigue' is now considered a common issue with using surveys, meaning that people grow tired of being asked to fill out quarterly, annual or pulse surveys.[55] In my experience, the limitation is less about fatigue and more about the frustration that accompanies filling out the survey, providing feedback only to find that little or nothing changes.

A helpful litmus test is if leaders dread sending out the new survey because they know they will need to admit nothing meaningful was done in response to the last survey.

I am currently coaching a leader who shared with me feedback posted in response to a qualitative question about a Mentimeter survey: 'What's the point asking us what we want to change or do better, when we see no one listening to our stated aspirations or acting in ways the company suggests we should be?' This sums up the frustration expressed by many people.

Often surveys spark new projects aimed at creating change when a more realistic manifestation of change would be seen in how leaders express aspired behaviours and bring them to life as part of their day-to-day activity and connections. Some of this is apparent in what leaders say, but they must also show it in what they do and how they do it.

A client recently told me that results from the company's most recent survey have been kept under a lid for fear of exposing a 20% drop in senior leadership confidence in the organisation's ability to cultivate changes to the conditions required for a new cohort of senior leaders purposefully hired from a variety of industries to drive cultural shifts supporting an explicit environmental, social and governance (ESG) strategic transformation.

Successfully integrating what people communicate in surveys entails creating space to listen. It also requires platforms to use the data to invite stories, allow opportunities to name and acknowledge what needs to change and highlight symbols of aspired change.

Let's say, for example, that a CEO gathers her 100 senior directors together for a culture transformation event and shares two insights from a recent survey:

1. The need for the creation of spaces where psychological safety is the normative condition.

2. A preference for leadership that encourages and celebrates learning from mistakes.

To practise what she preaches authentically, she could share a personal vulnerability with her leadership, such as a significant mistake she made that carries consequences she feels brave enough to face in the company of her colleagues, in a way that shows her fragility through open and raw emotion. Of course, this will only carry weight if it is true… Marrying leadership and culture together, the CEO demonstrates that she has listened by naming the change, embodying and reminding people of it, and then making it a repeatable process.

From disparate tribes to the 'Power of One' team

The five-year culture transformation journey by leading consumer products business Helen of Troy is a remarkable success on this front, so I recommend an episode of the Heidrick & Struggles leadership podcast in which they talk to the CEO of Helen of Troy, Julien Mininberg.[56]

Once a territorial leader, more vested in driving success of one of its business units during a time when the conglomerate (currently $2 billion NASDAQ) was growing through acquisition, Julien Mininberg shared the fundamental personal shift he had to make to his mindset to embrace the 'Power of One'. This was a concept created by his previously resistant leadership team to harness the collective and move away from a fragmented, siloed organisation.

The journey began with the formation of a 'council' whose mission was to create a strategic approach with a core cultural element – explicitly and carefully generating a set of values and behaviours for people to rally around and bring a two-phased strategic process to life. The first phase involved the council becoming a collective team with shared goals, motivations and collective leadership behaviours.

Mininberg shared his own shift in values and behaviours and the vulnerability he felt at having to let go. He and the council considered the 'shadow' that this new entity cast over the organisation and consciously made choices about what was 'permitted and promoted' in order to translate messages they communicated into genuine conversations where people could gradually transition away from low levels of engagement and hesitance. Despite communicating a new destination and route, the council consciously avoided expecting people to jump on board and instead adopted a more curious attitude about what it would mean to gently handhold and invite people to work out the journey with them and with each other.

The council developed into a leadership team that overtly chose to put the company first and depart from the individual 'tribes they each led'. People witnessed the shift in their leaders and felt able to follow them safely. Mininberg said he felt calm after he transmitted his power across his leadership team and their energy grew. The leadership team led a full overhaul of people processes, systems and organisational design. A standout in this case study is how the leadership took the bold decision to adapt the company's reward and recognition structure. They made *everyone* an owner, giving each employee fifty 'transformation' shares. They didn't expect people to just act like owners – they were and still are owners of the transformed brand and business.

Bedding down

Many years after the breastfeeding incident, the sense remains that my freedom to choose how and where I fed my baby was inhibited. Effects of this incident inevitably form threads in our cross-cultural family fabric. Tensions have resurfaced at times and these have triggered divisive undertones. This situation has made me aware that it may be impossible to fully disentangle some of these differences.

I realise that lived experience of conflict can stem from cultural differences. The ideas, customs and behaviours of a society different from mine form part of each environment I inhabit. A judgment about whether a request – like the one made to me not to breastfeed in the company of family members – is right or wrong, appropriate or inappropriate, acceptable or unacceptable, is underpinned by the cultural assumptions held when judging it. When I consider a systemic view of my family, I resist passing judgment and remain curious and accepting that there is simply a difference between us. But the emotional burden this carries is significant.

Being a third-culture child (one who has been raised in a different culture to that of my parents) has meant that I am not able to associate with a specific national identity. I'm not Venezuelan, Indian, American or British. As a mother, this also carries consequences, especially when it comes to the values, norms and culture I feel strongly about shaping as a parent in an environment reinforced by a dominant culture.

My children identify as British as my husband and I have chosen a life in the UK and to school them in the British education system. I accept the choices I have made, but this does not detract from the reality that it sometimes feels foreign to me. I am unable to identify with or model a culture that clearly and distinctly represents a culture we share. This can be a real source of discomfort and angst, which causes conflict and triggers emotions that others (especially those who form part of the dominant culture) cannot identify with. This dynamic can leave me feeling powerless or misunderstood. I remain on a journey of learning to reconcile and navigate this with humility and grace.

Although these may be profound examples, less extreme and more common cross-cultural forces impinge on personal values and norms in many day-to-day situations and organisations. These complex, and often problematic dynamics, can be painful. They stem from distinctions in cultures, values, norms, morals and behaviours, but they can equally present opportunities for better understanding and acceptance – necessary conditions for harnessing diversity and inclusion in any context.

My story shines a light on two contradictory drivers that I believe we all share as humans:

1. The desire to be uniquely our 'self'.

2. The need to be accepted, which can involve taking actions to conform.

There must be a mistake,
I need to fit in AND stand out

The moment I respected the request at that family gathering, I subconsciously favoured the second driver. If faced with this situation again, I would choose to meet both drivers. I would express my acknowledgement of the discomfort the family felt about me breastfeeding my son when they were present. To respect and honour their feelings, I would reassure them about the discreet way in which I would feed my son, given my modest Catholic and Muslim roots, but I would stress that being together would be something that benefitted us all.

In the final chapter, we will explore the possibilities created by noticing and exercising personal choice.

A SPACE FOR YOU TO REFRACT

1. What is the relevance of cultural difference in your life and your work context?

2. How has your awareness of cultural differences evolved over time?

3. What do you take away from this chapter about the sensitivities and challenges relating to cultural differences you encounter?

4. What are the implications of this for your team, functional and organisational context?

5. What assumptions might you need to surface and question to work more skilfully with those you don't share cultural similarities with?

6. Why might this be important?

8
Wielding Agency

Beaming a light to awaken you...

What serves you well within the environments in which you exist, by choice or otherwise, is within your gift to determine and repeatedly reinvent and change.

Gift of time and attention

It is strange, given my need for acceptance and belonging, but I have struggled to find the energy to maintain friendships in recent years. The irony is I have friends all over the world who are giving, caring and generous with their friendship, and they have shown me repeatedly how much I am loved. Some of these friends are attentive and in touch regularly, checking up on me and wanting to ensure I feel cared for. I experienced this to an inordinate level during Darshan's illness when the support was abundant.

Fraser has made me aware of a tendency to maintain a relatively isolated stance rather than reciprocating. Unfortunately, when we got back from the US where the final phase of Darshan's treatment took place, I experienced anger that I found difficult to express. I shared a public blog post about it after Darshan was cured:

> 'It's been difficult to connect with people
> recently. Uncomfortable emotions seem
> to envelop conversations. People ask how
> I am/how Darshan is. I either respond with
> a bland statement that things are fine now
> or they follow their question swiftly with
> their own interpretation. But it's not really
> a true reflection of the reality. When I have
> given a response about how Anees is doing—
> indicating few peaks and many longer
> troughs, a typical reaction is, 'Well if it's any
> consolation—my child has exactly the same
> ups and downs—so it's pretty normal.'[57]

Conversations triggered an explosive wave of resentment towards anyone who, despite positive intent and sympathy, failed to acknowledge the difference. A mixture of confusing emotions of guilt, shame and anger continued to bubble up and surface in the years that followed. I distanced myself from many of my friendships and social circles because it felt easier to avoid these situations than to be reminded about how broken I felt, how little I could relate to others and how derailed my life had become.

The pandemic made this avoidance easier. First, there was no need to see others socially and therefore less pressure to make the effort. Fraser admitted a similar feeling. He described our life that lacked social commitments but involved more intimate family time riding bikes, walking the beautiful landscape surrounding our home and chilling at home as calming and peaceful. Many people we knew seemed to have entered a state of hibernation during and in between lockdown periods. Second, I wonder whether the fact that everyone experienced disruption in their lives (and the world suffered a form of collective trauma) created more understanding and acceptance of reclusive behaviours.

I feel shame when I admit to myself that I am exercising free will to do what serves me best by choosing to withdraw from social connections with friends and family. I am fully aware that I risk failing to reciprocate my responsibility and role as a friend to those who have been generous and giving towards me and those who need care and support. I have also felt lonely and sad, and I realise that by making some of these choices I am alienating and hurting myself and potentially influencing my children in a way that could be detrimental.

Anees is blossoming as a young tween (a term used to describe a twelve-year-old in a world where kids are growing up at an unprecedented pace). The unfortunate timing of her move to a new school has, however, presented further adversities. We made the decision to move her to a new school a year earlier than most children move from primary to senior school. The new school is more suited to her dyslexia and, from an emotional perspective, offers a new environment where her identity is no longer associated with her brother's survival from cancer.

Good intentions aside, the move collided with the start of the pandemic, making it a distorted transition. Academically the school excels with specialist support that puts neurodivergent learning at the heart of how all pupils are taught. Socially, however, her integration has been less than ideal. Google Classroom online learning throughout lockdown was not conducive to making new friends. Intermittent returns to school involved social distancing. Pupils in naturally well-established friendship groups craved physical reconnection, making it hard for Anees to fit in.

The pubescent changes of a budding female teenager, which stimulate all sorts of physical and emotional developments, combined with the hazards inflicted by the world of social media make Anees' post-traumatic journey a priority for me. Frequent conversations together have revealed that, despite our childhood stories being so different, we share a similar experience of 'living on the sidelines'. Her observations, ability to question and the eloquence of her emotive expression are striking at her young age. It also makes it hard for her when many children her age lack the life experience and maturity to understand the strength of her emotional intelligence and wisdom.

We talk about dilemmas that I hope all mothers and daughters share as openly. We naturally have moments involving friction and conflict, but we talk. We might give each other space when angry, but we return to each other. Our evening meditations are a sanctuary of shared respite from the challenges life throws at us. I realise our mindful and therapeutic connection is rare, and I wish for it to endure the tests that it will face as Anees voyages through the hormonal changes and boundary setting that teenage girls traverse. I remain hopeful but realistic.

While writing this final chapter, Anees and I had a memorable conversation during which we talked about some of the rivalries and frictions she was experiencing in her school, which were having an impact on her self-esteem. She asked me what I cherish most about being a good friend and having close friends. I reflected on times when I felt closest with my friends (in middle school, high school, during university and as a fellow mother). I shared how it felt to be in their care and company – the companionship, unconditional love, feeling of being heard, permission to provoke and debate, trust that we would protect each other and the sensation of flow when we would forget about the rest of the world. Looking back, we gave each other the one gift we could never get back – time and attention.

In contrast, something that has become clear to me as life gets more complicated is how I cherish the freedom of space more than ever and yearn to elude judgment and the expectations of others that conflict with my needs, values and identity.

Anees and I explored how navigating this dilemma applies to friendship and life more broadly, and how there is a resource many (but admittedly not all humans) have access to that can be of help: personal choice.

The ingredients of a long and healthy life

Dan Buettner is the founder of Blue Zones®, a team of medical researchers, anthropologists, demographers and epidemiologists who over the last fifteen years have researched (and discovered) the five places or 'blue zones' on earth where people live the longest and healthiest lives.[58]

Blue zones have a large proportion of people who live to 100 years of age and people in their eighties and nineties who are active, fit and don't tend to suffer the degenerative illness that is so prevalent in the industrialised world. The blue zones include Ikaria, an island in Greece; Okinawa, an island in Japan; the Barbagia region of Sardinia in Italy; Loma Linda, a small city in California; and the Nicoya peninsula in Costa Rica.

The team found evidence-based causalities for good, long-term health, including the following:[59]

1. Regular physical movement

2. Clarity of personal purpose

3. Disciplines and routines aimed at maintaining healthy stress levels

4. Following the 80% rule (they stop eating when their stomachs are 80% full and eat less in the evening)

5. A 95% plant-based diet[60]

6. Consuming a moderate amount of wine in the company of friends and family

Besides the more physiological factors, they discovered three causes related to human connection and community:

1. A connection with a faith-based community

2. Having healthy close family connections

3. Having meaningful friendships and strong social networks

This study made me realise just how important Anees' question about what I cherish most about being a good friend and having close friends is and the implications for me and others.

Over the years (and since my journey involving paediatric cancer), I have prioritised what it takes to foster good health by gaining a better understanding of the aspects of healthy living relating to how I nourish my (and my family's) body through foods, routines, movement and by managing some sort of equilibrium between them. But the aspects of the blue zone research relating to stress levels, friends, family and faith provoked my curiosity about the choices we make in life – in a professional and wider context.

Learning from my mentors

I delight in memories of the work I have done with my mentors. This learning space is unusual in that it is gifted to me, but it is infused with incredible intuition from people who care for me.

It has led to me learning how to be honest with myself about my values and personal purpose. Inquiring into my life context over uninterrupted hour-long conversations enabled me to reflect on where I have come from and how I have progressed. This has also involved staying in the present and imagining the future – staying with the 'here and now' but also being decisive about goals and accountable by creating personal strategies to test. I have done, and continue to do, this work with the generous help of the following mentors, peers and others whose different perspectives and approaches inspire clarity but also challenge me to step out of my comfort zone:

- **Robin Ladkin**: my first mentor who helped me understand the roots and dynamics of my perfectionism in my early twenties – a red flag I needed to note and work with.

- **Kim De Morgan**: a friend and peer who helped me soften the entrenched value I placed on being an autonomous woman and resisting help from others.

- **Anthony Kasozi**: a mentor and peer who modelled and inspired in me the ability to question, translate and check my values as a woman and parent.

- **Simon Cavicchia**: my supervisor who enlightened me about a field with forces that I cannot see and will only access if I allow my full body to guide me. This involves senses beyond seeing and hearing and processes beyond thinking and feeling emotionally.

- **Jodi Cahill**: my tutor in Biomedicine who has taught me science and prescribed naturopathic remedies, helping me to understand causes and effects rooted in the belief that 'our body has a tremendous ability to heal itself' and that we can enhance the conditions for healing through natural means.

- **Eliat Aram**: the psychotherapist who created a space for me to understand my past, relish the gift of my emotional capacity and sieve my emotional surges with awareness, regulation and selective disclosure.

- **Alex Knight**: an early boss and mentor who showed me how to articulate dilemmas and paradoxes before taking me through what this means for others, organisations and business processes. I learned the language of logic from him.

- **Piero Dell'Anno**: my closest peer and best friend who interrupts and questions me, distorts my thinking, at times irritates and angers me but who also supports me with love when I am my own most crippling force.

There are others who have helped me refine my ability to recognise the 'personal agency' I claim and ensure I exercise in my life. They include conflictive relations, and I am grateful for the boundaries these situations have helped me set and use.

Personal agency

Agency is the belief in our capacity to act in (and have a sense of control over) a situation. The theory is that if I have the mindset that I can make a difference to the surrounding conditions and outcomes, I will be more motivated and incentivised to face the situation. But it is not as simple as it sounds.

'Self-efficacy' is a concept developed by psychologist Albert Bandura, professor of psychology at Stanford University, in the 1970s. Research into the understanding of personal agency has evidenced that self-efficacy is correlated with our perception of potential threats and how they are processed cognitively.[61] The implication is that if I believe I can address or manage a threat, I will experience less distress. Self-efficacy is believed to be developed through mastery (which evidences our ability to perform and achieve a result), through seeing others perform, especially when we can relate to them, through getting positive feedback and through another person's expression of belief in us.

Stephen Covey disseminated this concept more widely in his book *The 7 Habits of Highly Effective People*, first published in 1989.[62] He distinguished between 'proactive' people who focus on what they can do and influence and 'reactive' people who focus their energy on things beyond their control and blame the elements. Covey's model has enabled many individuals and teams to benefit from distinguishing between 'low hanging fruit' (what is within reach) and items that are far beyond our control and influence, such as the environmental consequences of our behaviour, societal attitudes and certain policies dictated by an organisation. The latter things are best left in what Covey calls a 'sphere of concern'. It is better to focus energy and attention on what people *can* influence, which enables them to make changes.

Covey's assumption is that our 'sphere of influence' is likely to increase, demonstrating our agency, effectiveness and power. Conversely, if our energy and attention are drained by the things we cannot influence, the impression others get is that we are less effective and disempowered.

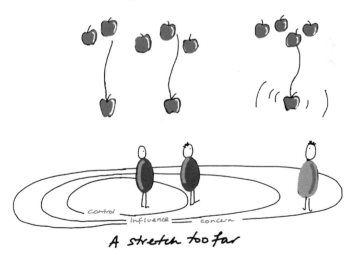

A stretch too far

Simple and easy to use, this model is practical in the short term and it may help individuals and teams become more empowered, but we live in a world where personal choice is becoming the norm rather than the exception. We are questioning what is right and what our needs are. There is more conversation about and encouragement to embrace the diversity of needs, preferences and learning styles and neurodiversity.

Has the pandemic awakened agency in more of us?

The human race is becoming more demanding. We expect more. The pandemic has given people a wake-up call and many are striving for more purposeful lives. I suspect this is the start of a new phase in which people's purposes become an equal force to profit and material reward. This is an encouraging development.

As Sri HWL Poonja (Papaji) said, 'If you are acting like a sheep, do not blame the shepherd. You cannot herd lions. Wake up and roar and you are free.'[63]

In the October to December quarter of 2021, the number of job vacancies in the UK rose to a record high of 1,247,000. This represented an increase of 462,000 from its pre-COVID level in January to March 2020, with most industries displaying record numbers of vacancies. From October to December 2021, the UK also reached a record ratio of 4.1 vacancies to every 100 jobs.[64]

The great resignation.
People want more from work

According to Rani Molla, 'Higher-paid workers are increasingly quitting their jobs, as the Great Resignation – also known as the Great Reshuffle – enters its second year.'[65] The demographic of those leaving organisations is changing from lower-paid industries like health and retail to more experienced and higher-paid industries like finance and tech. Company culture is no longer merely a 'nice-to-have' for the good, passionate and capable people organisations want to attract. It is a core criterion that employees use to judge opportunities along with salary, benefits and location. A desire for more meaning associated with the work people do and flexibility to work remotely are being prioritised.

At the time of writing this book, retaining talent is a tough challenge for many businesses. People are actively seeking and finding environments where their values, needs and ability to work and contribute without compromise are palpable. Employment opportunities are at record levels.

People question whether the work they do is meaningful, if their skills are being used, if they feel valued and whether their contribution is recognised. They ask themselves the following questions:

1. Why am I doing this?

2. What is it for?

3. How can my environment help me do better work?

4. What are the consequences of working in a toxic environment?

The answers to these questions are causing a growing number of people to lose faith in their leadership and to leave their jobs and organisations. This is having a disproportionate impact on competition for the best talent and the power is seemingly shifting in a way that is influenced by personal choices.

People are becoming empowered to take matters into their own hands to such an extent that the goals of financial performance and meeting the needs of employees now share paramountcy. In the spotlight are critical factors such as people feeling affinity with their organisation's purpose and vision, the ingredients for more collaboration and fewer territorial silos, an equitable workforce that demonstrates gender equality (through representation in numbers at all levels and supporting policies) and an organisational environment that proactively nurtures people's good health and wellbeing.

This appetite for change applies to leaders too. According to a report by global outplacement firm, Challenger, Gray & Christmas, US-based companies experienced a 38% increase in CEO departures between September and October 2021. This was also 54% higher than the number of CEOs who left their roles in the same month in 2020. In fact, it is the highest number of CEO exits in any month since January 2020. According to senior vice president Andy Challenger: 'Companies are trying to figure out new ways to convince people to stay, and part of that is asking them directly what's going to keep them in the job.'[66]

In 'stay interviews' aimed at responding to people's needs to try to convince them not to leave, employees (CEOs are no exception) who are moving companies or industries are reporting that, in addition to remuneration and benefits, disappointment with a company's culture is a key factor in their decision.

The complexity of moral injury

Studies led by Ludmila Praslova, a professor of Industrial/Organizational Psychology at Vanguard University of Southern California, link the great resignation trend to great disillusionment and its correlation with high levels of stress and anxiety.[67] People are increasingly seen to be leaving organisations, disillusioned and raising grievances. At the time of writing this chapter, I had four separate conversations with leaders who were personally involved in legal proceedings to defend themselves (representing their employer or business owners) against grievances. The message I heard was unanimous – these were highly stressful situations that caused sleepless nights and disruption to their work.

Efforts by organisations to enhance the employee experience by supporting employees on more personal challenges infused pandemic-related pressures, are driving what *Financial Times* feature writer Emma Jacobs calls 'a revolution in workplace culture leading to the rise and rise of what you might call the nanny employer'. Tactics made by employers categorically aiming to be more people-focused include offering paid time off, financial management training, mental health support including mindfulness apps and even more specific resources relating to the difficulties faced by women more openly talking about menopausal changes (fuelled by campaigns such as Davina McCall's #menopauserevolution).[68] Jacobs juxtaposes these gestures with the bleak reality that the primary interest of [most] employers is productivity and the pursuit of profit, validating this with results from a survey of FT readers revealing complaints that 'the language of empathy [does] not match reality'. A reduction in time and additional perks is not in any way proportionate to the volume of work and boundless expectations.[69]

Praslova discussed how early insights from research suggest that at least a quarter of people reporting burnout are actually victims of what she describes as 'moral injury', which is 'the strong cognitive and emotional response that can occur following events that violate a person's moral or ethical code.'[70] Moral injury is caused by a threat to one's personal ethics and values. Praslova argues that PTSD predominantly affects the sense of safety, burnout impacts one's sense of engagement and efficacy, but moral injury affects a person's sense of trust or self-respect. In my experience, ethical pressures that people and organisations are increasingly facing are due to conflicting demands – many of which are described in Chapter 3.

Although the concept of moral injury is historically associated with the military world, recent focus on the health sector has highlighted the sentiment of those clinicians working endlessly to deliver care during the pandemic with declining levels of resources and staffing. Dean and Talbot spoke in 2018 of a palpable tension clinicians at the front line grapple with involving 'the challenge of simultaneously knowing what care patients need but being unable to provide it due to constraints that are beyond our control'.[71] What is perceived as burnout, is anguish rooted in moral injury.

A study on the psychosocial impact of COVID on 4,378 UK healthcare staff reported 'higher exposure to moral injury (distress resulting from violation of one's moral code) was strongly associated with increased levels of common mental disorders (CMDs), anxiety, depression, PTSD symptoms and alcohol misuse.'[72] The study concluded with a call for further rigorous longitudinal studies to better understand and respond to potential longer-term mental health impacts stemming from the pandemic.

In my coaching work, a growing number of leaders are expressing a sense of resentment stemming from a feeling that their deeply held values are no longer in harmony with organisational narratives driven by financial success.

DETERMINATION DESPITE DISILLUSION

I recently coached a well-respected C-suite client leading a major digital implementation who is passionate about, as a minimum measure, propagating a sustainability paradigm within the organisation. At most, he is determined to fundamentally disrupt the corporate behaviour and practices of a growing number of corporate organisations to truly make a shift in service of the planet.

I sensed a pattern in our conversations indicating 'the leakage' of an emotion I could only label as disdain. He described how the business and leadership of his organisation are missing a trick in authentically aligning the organisation's espoused environmental, social and governance (ESG) intentions both internally as well as externally in its marketplace. Many times, he stressed how the emphasis of decision-making is on 'hitting the numbers' and this overshadows the imperative to generate great conditions for people, culture, ethics and values at a time when these characteristics are critical to attracting and retaining talent. I also noticed that despite the commitment and demonstrable action he craves from the leadership team of which he is a member, he continues to initiate (without much sponsorship or permission) tangible and measurable organisation-wide initiatives driving environmental consciousness and corporate social responsibility (CSR).

What strikes me most is the intensity of the negativity he tends to release at the start of our sessions, despite also sharing the incredible progress being made on all the ESG-related activity he spearheads. We talked about his need for this cathartic space, and he expressed how this helps him to calibrate his deeply held ethical values and how the obstacles and opposing forces within this environment impact his energy. It was also clear that, without more support, there will be a sell-by-date on his efforts given not only the limitations on what is achievable but also the cost to him of pushing a boulder up what feels like an endless hill. Philosophically, he shared a quote with me, 'Keeping one foot out the organisation at all times enables me to continue challenging the status quo.'

Handover all personal Values on entry

I recognise parallels between this story and Praslova's studies, in that the core of an individual's identity or self-concept can be rocked by factors in their surrounding environment that are at odds with them. What businesses and organisations espouse and the reality that employees and leaders experience diverge in many contexts. I am seeing more and more leaders and people stopping to question these inconsistencies and making the choice to no longer compromise.

The emotional cost, the likely 'disillusionment', and the existential and spiritual crises that result from these situations (which I'm seeing more in the individuals and teams I coach) may appear dramatic but, in the intimate quarters I share with people, the emotional releases are real and the effects are palpable and worrying. For example, Praslova talks about correlations or even causal relationships between moral injury and maladaptive behaviours, substance abuse and stress-induced physical illness.

Stress: a silent predator

My learnings about the mechanics of stress have alerted me to how grossly underestimated it is as a factor affecting the livelihood of so many of us.

Sympathetic dominance

Our nervous system contains a part that works without us having to think about it. This is called our autonomic nervous system: it comprises two branches, the 'parasympathetic' and 'sympathetic', each designed to meet different goals.

When it powers up, the sympathetic system activates stress hormones to increase the heart's contraction rate and body's alertness to help us combat threatening situations and do whatever it takes to survive. This system supports us through short-term, extreme levels of stress.

In contrast, the parasympathetic nervous system allows us to 'rest and digest' after the 'fight or flight' is over. It supports replenishment, growth and healing. It does this by enabling life-sustaining activities like digestion, blood flow and supply for our organs to function, and the production and distribution of hormones.

Growing levels of research validate the hypothesis that when we are 'sympathetic-dominant' and our nervous system is unbalanced, the sympathetic system becomes the primary control centre for our immediate thoughts, actions and responses. As a result, our health suffers. Symptoms and pathologies driven by sympathetic dominance include:

- Shoulder and neck muscle tightness

- Irritability

- Headaches

- Insomnia

- Fatigue

- Difficulty losing weight

- Hair loss

- High blood pressure

- Increased blood clotting factors and risk of deep vein thrombosis (DVT) and stroke

- Digestive problems: bloating, constipation or diarrhoea

- Hormonal imbalances including oestrogen dominance

- Gallbladder problems

- Uterine fibroids

- Thyroid imbalances

- Polycystic ovary syndrome (PCOS)

- Depression

Our genetics and environmental factors affect health. It is becoming increasingly clear that, for many pathologies, environmental factors play a bigger role than genetics. The field of study called 'epigenetics' demonstrates how environmental factors can turn genes on and off. Studies involving twins with a similar genetic predisposition for Type II diabetes in which one twin maintains healthy nutrition and physical exercise and invests in emotional wellbeing, while the other does the opposite, have proven that the latter's choices have led to the illness.

The World Health Organization (WHO) describes health as 'a state of complete physical, mental and social wellbeing and not merely the absence of disease or infirmity.'[73] Good health includes chemical, emotional or mental, and structural or physiological health – all of which require balance. An immense opportunity lies in the growing field of naturopathic and integrative medicine. Evidence shows that our bodies have a tremendous capacity for self-regulation and self-healing when nourishing conditions are created and maintained.

In Chapter 1, I shared the inevitable presence of traumas in our lives (those that might simply be a wound and those that are far more profound and detrimental), all of which carry the risk of pathological effects when stored and unprocessed. In Chapter 3, I talked about the realities we face in modern society that lead to a highly stressful life.

We live in a world where intrinsic drivers for personal ambition infuse organisational vision, where personal security and hygiene factors remain necessary conditions for life, and where unrelenting ambiguity and change are the only consistent conditions. All of these conditions and realities drive our autonomic nervous system to default to sympathetic dominance, where we are repeatedly in a state of high alert.

Creating an environment that counteracts the sympathetic system and disrupts our learned and automated responses (as described in more detail in Chapter 1) is critical to counterbalancing this force. A safe space is a vital requirement for individuals, organisational life and our day-to-day reality in teams. Our teams can interact and work using parasympathetic-infused patterns, rather than the 'firefighting' norms I see in many organisations. In a pandemic and post-pandemic world, the fully virtual and hybrid versions of working life add complexities to how we interact. We need to adapt to a new way of working besides the firefighting we have normalised as part of team and organisational life.

To disrupt this relentless and unquestioned dynamic, space, clarity, profound understanding and calm are essential. Only then can we rewire and work from a nonsympathetic-dominant stance in which 'calm' is our default.

Heart rate variability (HRV) – a meaningful measure

There is a need for a meaningful measurement method to help professionals engage with the nature of stress. I have recently begun a project involving the use of a heart-monitoring wearable device (Firstbeat) to track, measure and notice my stress patterns and ultimately gauge the state of my health.[74]

The wearable device helps increase our awareness of our overall health. By tracking and providing simple feedback, it can enable us to understand stress patterns, make easy and rapid corrective choices that impact those patterns, and importantly use real, current and focused data to move us from sympathetic-dominant patterns towards balancing the parasympathetic state. The desired and powerful effect is a transition towards more conscious, choiceful and better health.

Heart rate variability (HRV) is the variation in the time interval between consecutive heartbeats in milliseconds. This is different to our heart rate measured in beats per minute. A normal, healthy heart *does not* beat evenly – the rhythm is variable. HRV is regulated by the autonomic nervous system and is considered a noninvasive marker of autonomic nervous system activity. A high HRV level is considered an indicator of a healthy heart, reduced morbidity, and enhanced psychological health.

You can get a feel for your HRV by feeling the pulse on your wrist as you take a few deep breaths. The interval between beats elongates when you exhale and your heart rate slows down. The interval shortens when you inhale and your heart rate increases. So HRV is higher when our heart beats slowly and lower when our heart beats faster. In addition to breathing patterns, exercise, hormonal reactions, metabolic processes, cognitive processes, stress and recovery also influence HRV. When we face a stressor such as exercise or a distressing situation, our sympathetic nervous system is activated – this increases cardiac output, which decreases HRV.

HRV levels are correlated with our level of activity and stress. On a normal day, when the parasympathetic nervous system is dominant, HRV increases with relaxing activity like sleep or rest. During stressful periods, HRV decreases to cope with the additional demands placed on our bodies. When we are chronically stressed, our bodies default to the sympathetic-dominant fight state, accompanied by low HRV and the production of stress hormones like cortisol which, even when we rest and sleep, lead to many of the symptoms and secondary conditions I mentioned.

Genetic factors contribute to a mere 30% of HRV, validating that the potential for improvement through healthy lifestyle choices, stress management and exercise is significant.

Balancing my stress, recovery and self-care

My recent involvement in this heart-monitoring programme led me to train to use this device with leaders of a leading global pharmaceutical business to assess how stress plays a role in their health and performance. Using simple, indicative information in our coaching conversations, we aimed to directly influence personal choices that lead to better long-term health. Clients report gaining remarkable insights into more effective choices from this data.

Having used this myself as part of the training, I learned that specific choices I make around sleep (averaging eight hours per night), walks with my dogs out in natural surroundings and meditation practice mean I balance stress with recovery quite well. However, I also learned that I often choose to do high-intensity exercise late in the day. In addition to being aware that this is a sublimation on my part (an emotional defence mechanism we explored in Chapter 5), it degrades the quality of my sleep, adversely affects my ability to rest and replenish at night and undermines other good choices I make. As a result, I have now changed to doing high-intensity exercise earlier in the day to allow my body to make a more natural transition into a parasympathetic state at night. I am also more aware of the need to give myself a break and note the value of this.

The availability of methods for individuals to track and measure their health – from steps to calories to heart rate patterns – gives people the impetus to keep active. For example, the app *Strava* allows exercise junkies and extreme athletes to track bike and run segments, or there is expensive equipment like Peloton bikes and rowers that store data.

While many people use the software to push themselves and drive higher heart rate activity – assuming this maximises fitness and reduces weight loss – they miss an amazing opportunity to be more mindful of the time spent in a wider variety of more moderate heart rate zones, doing things like Pilates and stretching.

Like many high achievers, I am obsessed with data relating to my fitness activity. *MyZone*, a wearable tracker and app that my personal trainer Ben Rooney introduced me to, has encouraged my tendency towards addictive behaviour in a quest to score ever higher on their points system. I wore MyZone for yoga as well as for highly intensive activities and I grew frustrated with the lack of effort points I would earn. I realise now that I was driven by only one type of measurement which, on its own, undermines my overall health and wellbeing.

I have explored this pattern with Ben whose earlier years involved competitive boxing, a sport with a paradigm that entails winning at all costs. He shared how his journey from fighting to establishing a successful business that inspires a growing number of people to live a fit and healthy life involved a similar shift in mindset. He describes how, as a fighter, his toughest training sessions comprised sheer physical pain and unrelenting suffering, and were driven by a loud internal voice that dictated 'this is the difference between winning and losing'. During those competitive years, this supported his ambitions, but he needed to adjust his mindset to serve his changing life circumstances, choices and wellbeing including being a successful entrepreneur and family man.

I prioritised intensive exercise to become slimmer. I realise now that moderating stressors may actually slow my cortisol production and may even reduce the storage of excess fat around my waist and back. This is increasingly important as I am perimeno-pausal – and hormonal changes are even more likely to impact and be impacted by stressors through this transition. Yoga and other low-impact activity have the benefit of creating more parasympathetic time, which reduces stress and gives my body the time it needs to 'rest and digest'.

Although I am still learning to adjust to this para-digm shift, a new articulation of my physical health goal is: I am a fit, mobile, healthy-looking and feeling woman; I am doing what I can to minimise unwanted pathologies now and in the future and to live a long life. This means that scrutinising and feeling remorse about how this affects how slim or good I look are becoming secondary.

Bedding down

As I consider the inflexion points throughout my life and those still to come, a mounting sense of per-sonal agency fortifies the choices I make. I recognise that maturity and age contribute a great deal. I also have a clear conviction about being attentive to the following:

1. The values I commit to and live by.

2. The role my surrounding environment plays in supporting me.

3. How I prioritise my family (and gradually again my friendships).

4. What I am no longer prepared to give up or compromise, especially relating to the self-identity I have grown to accept and love.

5. The criticality of taking action to safeguard my health.

6. How worthwhile unleashing the energy that stems from my passions is.

7. Being kind and compassionate while also being aware of the shadow I cast (which is not something I can eliminate but is something I can carefully adjust).

I am aware that working on myself does not stop here. It is an interminable process of ongoing improvement which will, at times, feel pleasurable and rewarding and, at others, feel uncomfortable, frustrating and painful. The choices I make might carry consequences that affect the bigger picture and my relationships.

My continued willingness and efforts to explore, reframe and integrate the competing forces I shared throughout this book awaken me to the freedom and capabilities I possess.

A SPACE FOR YOU TO REFRACT

1. Which relationships – friendship and family – nourish you? Which relationship do you feel the need to reconsider or address and why?

2. Who has served as a mentor, guide or other influential figure, and how have these relationships supported your growth and development?

3. Consider your current context and explore to what extent you feel you have control and influence over factors impacting your life, work and destiny?

4. What criteria influence you to commit to staying in an organisation, and how decisive are you about these?

5. How are your values nourished or undermined by your workplace environment?

6. What word would you use to describe how you feel about the organisation you work within/ for? How do you feel thinking about this?

7. What are the health implications of your stress load?

8. How conscious are you of the consequences of this stress?

9. What can you do to take more control of the conditions that impact your health and resilience now and in the future?

Final Points

Common rhetoric I hear frequently is 'bring your whole self to work'. Nervously, I recognise that, by sharing insights into my *whole* self, this book does just that. This book is a public representation of my truths (bright and dark), my painful realities and my raw vulnerabilities.

This book shares stories of clients I have coached who also reveal moments, learning and adversities that inhabit their 'shadow' (a place not many see with the naked eye, but the effects of which are felt and experienced).

By creating safe spaces for myself and my clients, I allow for catharsis, the release of built-up emotions, the acknowledgement of the importance of this work, and I help to surface the resulting stress often accompanying this. This is a development process psychoanalysts Winnicott and Bion introduced in the 1960s using terms such as 'containment' and 'holding environment', which they believed to originate in the mother-child reciprocal exchange. This is where the mother is able to play the role of a 'container' within which she holds, processes and tolerates the child's emotional displays) and where the child is offered presence, patience and acceptance.[75]

Through my education and therapeutic support I have had the benefit of this process for my own work and healing. I am privileged to generate a similar type of 'containment' with clients and witness their awakening, learning and a transition towards agency and resilience when we work in this unique space together.

My intention in writing this book is to balance what is real and uncomfortable with what is constructive and enabling; to celebrate the major hurdles and the triumphs; to find and cherish learning even in the event of trauma; to become increasingly aware of the importance of this work for health and livelihoods, and to grow and become more resourceful no matter what happens.

An invitation to you

In this book, I invite you to be curious about the work I do with myself and clients. I offer as examples the ideas, theories, research and practices that frame and underpin how I make sense of, embrace and heal from the adversities that have shaped my life. I introduce the practice of 'refraction', equipping you with a novel frame and approach to slow down, change direction and generate greater visibility.

I cherish the possibility of readers taking inspiration and doing some of this work for themselves – seeing the unconscious demands upon us in today's world, being open to looking at themselves, venturing deeper and exploring what is not obvious to see. I invite you to explore ways that help you access embodied visceral insights. Our bodies have the immense capacity to reveal signs that offer ways for us to make sense of it all.

This book encourages leaders and team members in organisations to not only examine themselves introspectively, but to open their senses to the backdrop – the bigger picture, the whole system, and the subtle connections that exist to see, feel and think differently. To broaden and flex their perspectives by taking more interest in noticing the connections we form.

We have explored the lenses of our mammalian roots and the evolution and diverse aspects of psychological theory and practice. We have taken a closer look at the neuroscience of our threat response during times of distress, as well as how humans navigate an organisational setting, co-existing cultures and how we are affected by goals, intents, diverse needs, interests, roles, metrics and the pursuit of profit.

I put forth the argument that there is a clear and strong relationship between how we navigate life, past, present and future, and the less obvious physiology of our bodies and our health. This topic is at the heart of my future learning, as I strongly believe that we are already paying a big price for the lack of integration between these elements.

I have shared stories from my personal and professional life, which are both firmly integrated and impossible to separate. I have been told I am seen as the same person regardless of my environment, whether work, family or social, and I welcome that observation as a sign that I show up as my authentic self despite my struggles. The extent to which I speak up about a comment or behaviour that goes against my values or beliefs is consistent, whether I am speaking to a family member, a boss or a client. People say they see me as honest and courageous, with good intentions even during tricky conversations and interactions. This makes me happy.

What greater joy and freedom is there than to be your true and whole self?

A SPACE FOR YOU TO REFRACT

1. What has reading this book awakened in you?
2. What refractions are you seeing, sensing and feeling?
3. Is there someone impacted by your leadership you are moved to share this awakening with, and why?

Acknowledgements

I would like to acknowledge:

Darshan and Anees, for your curiosity about my passion for learning and humanity. Our dog walks… the stories you volunteer, the ideas you explore and your readiness to share have enabled me to clarify what I express in this book to reach many more willing learners. Darshan, you embody humble resilience; Anees, you personify raw vulnerability. Thank you for allowing me to share our stories of adversity so others can learn, develop and grow.

Fraser, words cannot express my gratitude to you for creating the conditions for me to bring this idea to fruition and for engaging in this work with me over the last two decades as my husband, friend, guide and challenger.

Suhail, mom and Shabbab, for the unfathomable time, space and scrutiny you have granted me throughout life and my journey writing this book. The challenges I express relating to my identity and culture may have been tough for you to read. I treasure your unconditional appreciation, judgment-free values and generosity for supporting me to share my stories to help others who have also endured the effects of a less conventional upbringing in a world that is growing in diversity.

Rachel Henke, for helping me to turn an idea into reality – for filling me with self-belief, holding me to account and enabling me to speak up about a topic that I passionately believe is so important to make this world a better place. Thank you for helping me to translate it for leaders by creating a relatable, catalytic and hopefully nourishing resource.

Candy Perry, for your unparalleled ability to express concepts that I want people to understand in a way that activates visceral responses is extraordinary. I love your provocations aimed at helping me project my voice with clarity and authority.

Kate Latham, and to Joe Gregory and the rest of the Rethink team who have patiently, and with care, guidance and flexibility, supported me to produce this book.

Melissa Sathria, for your unconditional support and the time and space you created for me to be able to produce this book and maximise my time doing the work I love – impacting clients' lives.

Those who have shone a light on the gift I bring to the world, through the guidance, supervision, mentoring and companionship you've given me at pivotal times in my life and profession: Simon Cavicchia, Piero Dell'Anno, John Higgins, Jodi Cahill, Loraine McSherry, Anthony Kasozi, Remi Olajoyegbe, Adam Pacey, Sarah Ives, Kim De Morgan, Laura Heath, Lindsey Masson, Steve Grant, Efrat Goldratt-Ashlag, Robin Ladkin, Claudia Heimer and Alex Knight.

Every client who has offered me the privilege of doing this work with you, for your trust, courage, growth mindset, diligence and for the insights and shifts we have generated together. You have all enriched me with a thirst to expand the transformation you have made to a wider community of leaders and people.

Peer practitioners out there, you perform this important work in intimate spaces behind the scenes and you give a lot of yourselves in the process. You create a safe space in which leaders, teams and organisations can pause, notice, question, feel, sense and shift their mindsets. You stimulate change in the systems they inhabit and help them learn and adopt skills and capabilities and adjust their behaviours based on more conscious choices. This transforms the conditions for the work that humans and organisations must do to create positive and purposeful change.

There are so many more people who have sewn threads into the fabric of my life and vocation. You know who you are, and I thank you so much for what you have given me.

References

1. G Gianasso, 'Emma Raducanu and the Illusion of Nations' (LinkedIn, 2022) www.linkedin.com/feed/update/urn:li:ac tivity:6844951439719190528
2. American Psychological Association, 'Trauma' (APA, nd), www.apa.org/topics/trauma
3. G Maté interviewed by C Jackson, 'Healing the Wounds of Trauma', (Therapy Today, September 2020)
4. RC Kessler, 'Trauma and PTSD in the WHO World Mental Health Surveys', *European Journal of Psychotraumatology*, 8: sup5 (2017), https://doi.org/10.1080/20008198.2017.1353383
5. B Paley and NJ Hajal, 'Conceptualizing Emotion Regulation and Coregulation as Family-Level Phenomena', *Clin Child Fam Psychol Rev* (2022); 25(1) 19–43 www.ncbi.nlm.nih.gov/pmc/articles/PMC8801237/
6. R Janoff-Bulman, 'Assumptive Worlds and the Stress of Traumatic Events: Applications of the schema construct'. *Social Cognition*, 7(2) (1989), 117. https://doi.org/10.1521/soco.1989.7.2.113
7. J Bowlby, 'Attachment and Loss: Attachment (Vol. 1)' (Basic Books, 1969); and JR Harris, *The Nurture Assumption: Why children turn out the way they do* (Free Press, 1998)

8. J Tierney and RF Baumeister, *The Power of Bad: How the negativity effect rules us and how we can rule it* (Penguin Press, 2019)
9. J Panksepp and L Given, *The Archaeology of the Mind: Neuroevolutionary origins of human emotions* (WW Norton & Co, 2012)
10. G Maté, *When the Body Says No: The cost of hidden stress* (Vermilion 2019)
11. Center on the Developing Child, 'ACEs and Toxic Stress: Frequently asked questions' (Harvard University, nd), https://developingchild. harvard.edu/resources/aces-and-toxic-stress-frequently-asked-questions
12. 'OECD Policy Responses to Coronavirus (COVID-19): Tackling the mental health impact of the Covid-19 Crisis' (OECD, 2021) www.oecd.org/coronavirus/policy-responses/tackling-the-mental-health-impact-of-the-covid-19-crisis-an-integrated-whole-of-society-response-0ccafa0b
13. OECD, 'Tackling Coronovirus (COVID-19): Contributing to a global effort (2021). https://read.oecd-ilibrary.org/view/?ref=1094_1094455-bukuf1f0cm&
14. L Campbell, 'The World Is Experiencing Mass Trauma From COVID-19: What you can do' (Healthline, 8 September 2020)
15. B van der Kolk, *The Body Keeps the Score: Brain, mind, and body in the healing of trauma* (Viking, 2014)
16. C Risen, 'Mihaly Csikszentmihalyi, the Father of Flow, Dies at 87' (*New York Times*, 2021) www.nytimes.com/2021/10/27/science/mihaly-csikszentmihalyi-dead.html
17. S Abuhamdeh and M Csikszentmihalyi, 'The Importance of Challenge for the Enjoyment of Intrinsically Motivated, Goal-directed Activities', *Personality and Social Psychology Bulletin*, 38, 317–330. https://doi.org/10.1177/0146167211427147
18. W Bennis and B Nanus, *Leaders: The strategies for taking charge* (Harper & Row, 1985)
19. S Fleming, 'This is the World's Biggest Mental Health Problem – and You Might Not Have Heard of It' (World Economic Forum, 14 January 2019), www.weforum.org/agenda/2019/01/this-is-the-worlds-biggest-mental-health-problem
20. AH Maslow, 'A Theory of Human Motivation', *Psychological Review*, 50(4) (1943), 370–396
21. T Eurich, *Insight: The surprising truth about how others see us, how we see ourselves, and why the answers matter more than we think* (Crown Business, 2017)

22. BL Brown, *Atlas of the Heart: Mapping meaningful connection and the language of human experience* (Random House, 2021)

23. Plato, *Charmides* (translated into English by B Jowett, 1870)

24. G Maté, *When the Body Says No: The cost of hidden stress* (Vermilion, 2019)

25. CJ Dahl, A Lutz and RJ Davidson, 'Reconstructing and Deconstructing the Self: Cognitive mechanisms in meditation practice', *Trends in Cognitive Sciences*, 19(9) (201), 515–23, https://doi.org/10.1016/j.tics.2015.07.001

26. Y Singh, A Goel, R Kathrotia and PM Patil, 'Role of Yoga and Meditation in the Context of Dysfunctional Self: A hypothetico-integrative approach', *Advances in Mind-Body Medicine*, 28(3) (2014), 22–5

27. BPS, *What is Psychology?*, www.bps.org.uk/public/what-is-psychology

28. Aristotle, B Jowett and HWC Davis, *Aristotle's Politics* (Clarendon Press, 1920)

29. MD Lieberman, *Social: Why our brains are wired to connect* (OUP, 2013)

30. J Bowlby, *Attachment and Loss: Vol. 1. Attachment* (Basic Books; 1969/1982)

31. C Hazan and PR Shaver, 'Romantic Love Conceptualized as an Attachment Process', *Journal of Personality and Social Psychology*, 52 (1987), 511–24

32. Cited in R Bailey and J Pico, 'Defense Mechanisms', *StatPearls* (2022), www.ncbi.nlm.nih.gov/books/NBK559106

33. JZ Muller, *The Tyranny of Metrics* (Princeton University Press, 2018)

34. R Goldratt, 'Management Attention: The ultimate constraint' (YouTube, 2018) www.youtube.com/watch?v=0DrMN8AN2HQ

35. A Sood and DT Jones, 'On Mind Wandering, Attention, Brain Networks, and Meditation', Explore (NY), 9(3) (2013 May-June), 136–41, https://doi.org/10.1016/j.explore.2013.02.005

36. S-Y Tsai et al, 'Meditation Effects on the Control of Involuntary Contingent Reorienting Revealed with Electroencephalographic and Behavioral Evidence', *Frontiers in Integrative Neuroscience*, 12: 17 (15 May 2018), https://doi.org/10.3389/fnint.2018.00017

37. MM Reitz et al, 'The Mindful Leader: Developing the capacity for resilience and collaboration in complex

times through mindfulness practice' (Hult Research, November 2016), https://static1.squarespace.com/static/597729cbcf81e0f87c7f6c61/t/5bb767c2eef1a11ad2b1d5 3c/1538746308010/Mindful-Leader-Report-2016-updated.pdf

38. G Morgan, *Images of Organization* (SAGE Publications, 2006)
39. J Lurie, 'Apply a Systemic Lens and Change your Business Perspective for the Better', (Kochie's Business Builders, 11 January 2019), www.kochiesbusinessbuilders.com.au/apply-a-systemic-lens-and-change-your-business-perspective-for-the-better
40. RD Stacey, 'The Science of Complexity: An alternative perspective for strategic change processes', *Strategic Management Journal*, 6:6 (1995), 477–495, https://doi.org/10.1002/smj.4250160606
41. S Western, *Leadership: A critical text* (SAGE Publications Limited, 2019)
42. J Marmorstein, *The Persistence of Psychoanalysis in the CyborgOrg*, Part II (CyorgORG, 2 February 2018), https://cyborgorg.net/2018/02/02/the-persistent-importance-of-psychoanalysis-in-the-cyborgorg-part-ii, accessed 13 December 2021
43. MG Dietz (ed), *Thomas Hobbes and Political Theory* (University Press of Kansas, 1990)
44. RM Emerson, 'Power-dependence Relations', *American Sociological Review* 27:1 (February 1962), 31–41, https://doi.org/10.2307/2089716
45. S Western and J Lurie, 'Edgy Ideas: Episode 31 – Organisational Ecology With Joan Lurie', https://open.spotify.com/episode/7tWvQlFeVzLWi21A9hlstn?si=uDGCj0RzTmOLT1kn27M_5g
46. M Heidegger, *Being and Time* (trans. by J Macquarrie and E Robinson), (Blackwell Publishing, 1978)
47. H García and F Miralles, *Ikigai: The Japanese secret to a long and happy life* (Hutchinson, 2017)
48. 'Global Culture Survey 2021' (PwC, 2021) www.pwc.com/gx/en/issues/upskilling/global-culture-survey-2021/global-culture-survey-2021-report.html
49. E Schein, *Organizational Culture and Leadership* (Jossey-Bass,1985)
50. R Hastings speech, www.slideshare.net/reed2001/culture-1798664
51. J Roettgers, 'How Netflix Ticks: Five key insights from the company's new corporate culture manifesto' (*Variety*, 2017)

https://variety.com/2017/digital/news/netflix-company-culture-document-1202474529

52. K Paul, 'Netflix Lays Off 300 Employees in Second Round of Job Cuts' (*The Guardian*, 23 June 2022), www.theguardian.com/media/2022/jun/23/netflix-layoff-300-employees-second-round-job-cuts

53. DHL, 'DHL is one of the world's best workplaces recognized by Great Place to Work®' (DHL.com, nd) www.dhl.com/global-en/home/press/press-archive/2019/dhl-is-one-of-the-worlds-best-workplaces-recognized-by-great-place-to-work.html

54. Zoom, 'Zoom's Customer-Centric Culture', (Zoom Blog, 2 June 2015) https://blog.zoom.us/zooms-customer-centric-culture

55. A DiLeonardo, 'Survey Fatigue? Blame the leader, not the question' (McKinsey, 2021), www.mckinsey.com/business-functions/people-and-organizational-performance/our-insights/the-organization-blog/survey-fatigue-blame-the-leader-not-the-question

56. C Carr, 'The Power of One: Helen of Troy's culture transformation journey' (Heidrick & Struggles, 2019), www.heidrick.com/en/insights/podcasts/episode_28_the_power_of_one_helen_of_troys_culture_transformation_journey

57. 'Darshan Fights Cancer', https://darshanfightscancer.wordpress.com/2018/03/29/tattoo/#more-2936

58. Blue Zones®, www.bluezones.com/live-longer-better

59. D Buettner, '9 Lessons from the World's Blue Zones on Living a Long, Healthy Life' (World Economic Forum, 2017), www.weforum.org/agenda/2017/06/changing-the-way-america-eats-moves-and-connects-one-town-at-a-time

60. R Robertson, 'Why People in "Blue Zones" Live Longer than the Rest of the World' (Healthline, 2017), www.healthline.com/nutrition/blue-zones

61. A Bandura, 'Personal and Collective Efficacy in Human Adaptation and Change', in J G Adair, D Belanger & K L Dion (Eds), *Advances in Psychological Science: Vol. 1. Personal, Social and Cultural Aspects* (pp. 51–71) (Psychology Press, 1998)

62. SR Covey, *The 7 Habits of Highly Effective People: Powerful lessons in personal change* (Simon & Schuster UK, 1999)

63. C Titmuss, 'An Interview with Sri H.W.L Poonjaji' (30 January 1991), http://papaji.hu/wp-content/uploads/2019/10/interview.pdf

64. 'Vacancies and Jobs in the UK: January 2022' (Office for National Statistics, 2022), (www.ons.gov.uk/employmentandlabourmarket/peopleinwork/employmentandemployeetypes/bulletins/jobsandvacanciesintheuk/january2022

65. R Molla, 'The Great Resignation is Becoming a "Great Midlife Crisis"', Vox, www.vox.com/recode/23042785/the-great-resignation-older-tenured-higher-paid

66. 'October 2021 CEO Turnover Report: The Great Resignation hits the top spot' (Challenger, Gray & Christmas, Inc, 22 November 2021), www.challengergray.com/blog/october-2021-ceo-turnover-report-the-great-resignation-hits-the-top-spot

67. LM Praslova, 'Feeling Distressed at Work? It might be more than burnout' (Fast Company, 14 January 2022), www.fastcompany.com/90712671/feeling-distressed-at-work-it-might-be-more-than-burnout, accessed 15 January 2022

68. 'The Menopause Revolution' (Positive Pause, nd), www.positivepause.co.uk/all-blogs/The%20Menopause%20Revolution

69. E Jacobs, 'Have We Had Enough of the Nanny Employer?' (*Financial Times*, 2022), www.ft.com/content/0506901f-d2a9-45bb-8a79-5ceb202e1675

70. V Williamson, D Murphy et al, 'Moral Injury: The effect on mental health and implications for treatment', *The Lancet*, 8/6 (2021), 453–455, https://www.thelancet.com/journals/lanpsy/article/PIIS2215-0366(21)00113-9/fulltext

71. SG Talbot and W Dean, 'Physicians Aren't "Burning Out": They're suffering from moral injury', STATREPORTS, 2018, www.statnews.com/2018/07/26/physicians-not-burning-out-they-are-suffering-moral-injury

72. D Lamb, S Gnanapragasam et al, 'The Psychological Impact of the COVID-19 Pandemic on 4,378 UK Healthcare Workers and Ancillary Staff', *Occupational and Environmental Medicine*, 2021, doi: 10.1136/oemed-2020-107276

73. 'Constitution of the World Health Organization' (World Health Organization, nd), www.who.int/about/governance/constitution

74. T Hoffman, 'What Is Heart Rate Variability (HRV) & Why Does It Matter?' (Firstbeat, nd), www.firstbeat.com/en/blog/what-is-heart-rate-variability-hrv

75. JS Grotsein, 'A Beam of Intense Darkness: Wilfred Bion's legacy to psychoanalysis' (Routledge, 2007)

The Author

As a daughter, parent, entre-preneur, executive coach, advisor and global citizen, Samreen draws upon a rich and diverse tapestry of tangible experience to generate distinctive insight into what it really takes to succeed as an authentic leader without compromise.

Going far beyond checklists of 'do's and don'ts' deficient in context, her customised and deeply profound work has catalysed thousands of individuals and teams worldwide to truly and deliberately harness more of their 'whole' selves in their role as a leader and contribution as a team.

Working with countless household name brands throughout a 25-year career, Samreen is passionate about those she works with, directly and via this book. Her interventions lead to extraordinary step-changes in their performance as leaders and individuals without needing to accept personal self-sacrifice to do so, directly benefiting organisations systemically.

Half Venezuelan and half Indian, Samreen has lived, studied and worked in Latin America, the US and Europe. She holds a BA in Political Science, MSc in Business Systems Analysis and Design, and PGDip in Counselling and Psychotherapy, and is a Hult Ashridge accredited coach and a trained practitioner of Dr Eli Goldratt's Theory of Constraints. Professionally trained in Organisational Behaviour and Systems Thinking during her time at Hult Ashridge business school, with further development from Metanoia Institute, Samreen continues to extend her repertoire into Naturopathic Medicine practices to more consciously facilitate the health and wellbeing of leaders and organisational cultures.

Samreen, her husband, two children and two very energetic dogs live on the outskirts of London, England, where she balances her academic and professional pursuits with her commitment to making choices that promote good health, a love of travel, photography and writing.

🌐 https://turmericgroup.com

💼 @SamreenMcGregor